AF437816

THE NEW-ENGLAND PRIMER COLLECTION

THE ABC BOTH IN LATIN AND IN ENGLISH

THE
New-England
PRIMER

Collection [1690–1843]

to which is added,

THE

ABC

Both in Latin & in English [1538]

ALEXANDRIA: Sold by the Booksellers.
Copyright 2020 by *Pinch Village, LLC.*

Contents

From A Guide For The Child & Youth (1725).

From The New England Primer (1727).

From The New England Primer (1737).

From The Royal Primer (1750).

From The New England Primer (1762).

From The New England Primer (1767).

From The New England Primer (1775).

From The New England Primer (1777).

From The New England Primer (1785).

From The New England Primer (1785-1790).

From The New England Primer (1787-1798).

From The New England Primer (1812).

From The New England Primer (1843).

THE ABC PRIMER

¶ The ABC Both In Latin And In English (1538).

FOREWORD.

THe following pages contain a near-exhaustive collection of excerpts from two notable primers in the English language: THE ABC BOTH IN LATIN AND IN ENGLISH and THE NEW ENGLAND PRIMER. The use of such primers was, as the name implies, educational. They were to be the first books placed in the hands of children and to contain all that was necessary for them to understand the rudiments of the English language and participate in the activities of their local church.

THE ABC BOTH IN LATIN AND IN ENGLISH was published around 1538 by Thomas Petit in London. It is the earliest known specimen of primers containing the English alphabet and the prayers and elementary religious formularies used in the teaching of children and the daily life of home.

THE NEW ENGLAND PRIMER was first printed around 1690 by Benjamin Harris in Boston and went through innumerable editions. It reflected in a marvelous way the spirit of the age that produced it, and contributed, perhaps more than any other book except the Bible, to the moulding of those sturdy generations that gave to America its liberty and its institutions.

This volume consists of two sections. The first larger section is an attempt by the editors to include, so far as is possible, an example of every text published in the various editions of THE NEW ENGLAND PRIMER between between the years 1690 and 1843. Each piece is classed under the primer (or prototype) in which it first appeared.

The concluding section presents THE ABC BOTH IN LATIN AND ENGLISH in its entirety. For improved readability, separate fonts have been used for Latin and English words. Where missing, translations are provided in the footnotes.

THE NEW-ENGLAND PRIMER COLLECTION

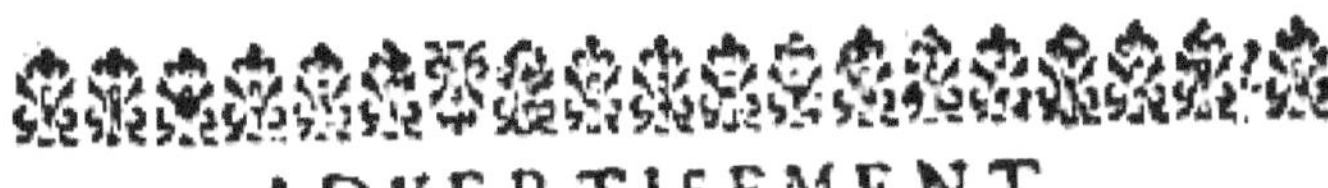

ADVERTISEMENT.

There is now in the Press, and will suddenly be extant, a Second Impression of *The New-England Primer enlarged*, to which is added, more *Directions for Spelling* : the *Prayer of* K. *Edward* the 6*th*. and *Verses made by Mr.* Rogers *the Martyr, left as a Legacy to his Children.*

Sold by *Benjamin Harris*, at the *London Coffee-House* in *Boston*.

a b c d e f g h i j k l m
n o p q r s t u v w x y z
Vowels.
A E I O U Y   a e i o u y
Consonants.
b c d f g h j k l m n p q r s t v w x z
Double Letters.
ff ss st fi si sh fl sl ffi ssi ffl et
Italick Letters.
Aa Bb Cc Dd Ee Ff Gg Hh Ii
Ji Kk Ll Mm Nn Oo Pp Qq Rr
Ss Tt Uu Vv Ww Xx Yy Zz
Italick Double Letters
ff ss fi si sh st fl sl ffl ffi ssi et

The Great English Letters,

𝔄 𝔅 ℭ 𝔇 𝔈 𝔉 𝔊 ℌ 𝔍
𝔍 𝔎 𝔏 𝔐 𝔑 𝔒 𝔓 𝔔
ℜ 𝔖 𝔗 𝔘 𝔚 𝔛 𝔜 𝔷.

The Small English Letters.

a b c d e f g h i j k l m n
o p q r r s s t u w x y z.

Great Letters.

A B C D E F G H I J K L M N
O P Q R S T U V W X Y Z.

Easie Syllables For Children.

ab	eb	ib	ob	ub
ac	ec	ic	oc	uc
ad	ed	id	od	ud
af	ef	if	of	uf
ag	eg	ig	og	ug
ak	ek	ik	ok	uk

From The New England Primer (1690).

al	el	il	ol	ul
am	em	im	om	um
an	en	in	on	un
ap	ep	ip	op	up
ar	er	ir	or	ur
as	es	is	os	us
at	et	it	ot	ut
ax	ex	ix	ox	ux
ba	be	bi	bo	bu
ca	ce	ci	co	cu
da	de	di	do	du
fa	fe	fi	fo	fu
ga	ge	gi	go	gu
ha	he	hi	ho	hu
ka	ke	ki	ko	ku
la	le	li	lo	lu
ma	me	mi	mo	mu
na	ne	ni	no	nu
pa	pe	pi	po	pu
ra	re	ri	ro	ru
sa	se	si	so	su
ta	te	ti	to	tu

Words Of One Syllable.

Are	be	child	face
air	best	clay	fine
add	bed	cry	fair
all	hold	cup	few
ape	bad	ear	fight
God	kid	grace	give
great	kind	heart	hat
grant	kill	had	hath
good	kick	goose	glass
grass	kiss	hair	he
grow	knee	head	health
heal	long	nine	peace
how	man	no	peep
hide	maid	nose	pence
knit	mole	of	pitch
known	moon	old	play
knew	more	once	pure

Words Of Two Syllables.

Ab-sent	Absent
Bold-ly	Boldly
Con-stant	Constant
De-pend	Depend
En-close	Enclose
Fa-ther	Father
Glo-ry	Glory
Hus-band	Husband

Words Of Three Syllables.

A-bu-sing	Abusing
Be-witch-ing	Bewitching
Con-found-ed	Confounded
Drun-ken-ness	Drunkenness
E-ras-mus	Erasmus
Fa-cul-ty	Faculty
God-li-ness	Godliness
Ho-li-ness	Holiness
Im-pu-dent	Impudent
Ka-len-der	Kalender.

Words Of Four Syllables.

Ac-com-pa-ny	Accompany
Be-ne-vo-lence	Benevolence
Ce-re-mo-ny	Ceremony
Dis-con-tent-ed	Discontented
E-ver-last-ing	Everlasting
Fi-de-li-ty	Fidelity
Glo-ri-fy-ing	Glorifying
Hu-mi-li-ty	Humility
In-fir-mi-ty	Infirmity.

Words Of Five Syllables.

Ad-mi-ra-ti-on	Admiration
Be-ne-fi-ci-al	Beneficial
Con-so-la-ti-on	Consolation
De-cla-ra-ti-on	Declaration
Ex-hor-ta-ti-on	Exhortation
For-ni-ca-ti-on	Fornication
Ge-ne-ra-ti-on	Generation
Ha-bi-ta-ti-on	Habitation
In-vi-ta-ti-on	Invitation

A · In *Adam's* Fall
We Sinned all.

B · Thy Life to Mend
This *Book* Attend.

C · The *Cat* doth play
And after stay.

D · A *Dog* will bite
A Thief at night.

E · An *Eagles* flight
Is out of sight.

F · The Idle *Fool*
Is whipt at School.

G As runs the *Glass*
Mans life doth pass.

H My Book and *Heart*
Shall never part.

J *Job* feels the Rod
Yet blesses GOD.

K Our *King* the good
No man of blood.

L The *Lion* bold
The *Lamb* doth hold.

M The *Moon* gives light
In time of night.

N　*Nightingales* sing
In Time of Spring.

O　The Royal *Oak*
it was the Tree
That sav'd His
Royal Majestic.

P　*Peter* denies
His Lord and cries.

Q　*Queen* Esther comes
in Royal State
To Save the JEWS
from dismal Fate

R　*Rachel* doth mourn.
For her first born.

S　Samuel anoints
Whom God appoints

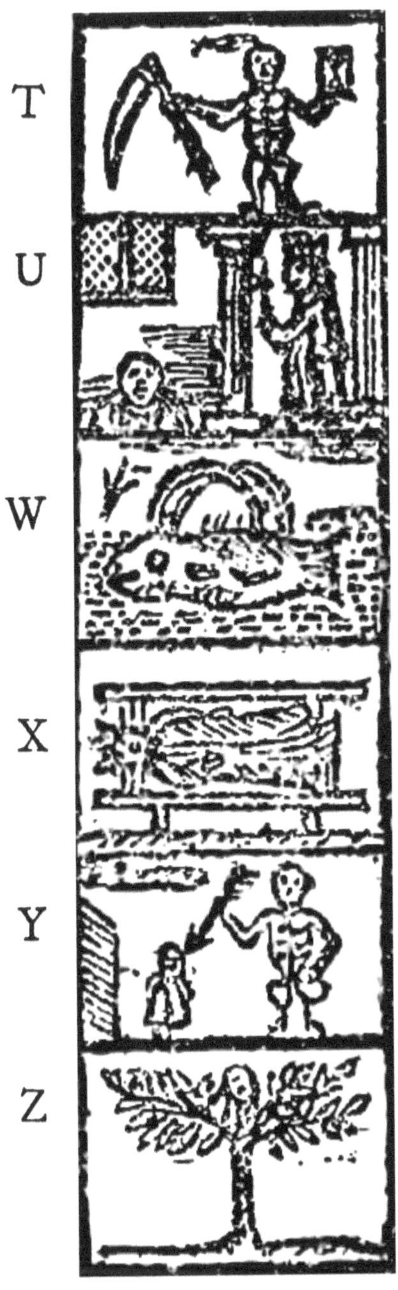

T	*Time* cuts down all Both great and small.
U	*Uriah's* beauteous Wife Made David seek his Life.
W	*Whales* in the Sea God's Voice obey.
X	*Xerxes* the great did die, And so must you & I.
Y	*Youth* forward flips Death soonest nips
Z	*Zacheus* he Did climb the Tree. His Lord to see.

The Prayer Of King Edward The Sixth.

Ord, God, deliver me out of this miserable and wretched Life, take me among thy Chosen, how be it not my Will, but thy Will be done. Lord, I commit my Spirit to thee : O Lord, thou knowest how happy it were for me to be with thee, yet for thy Chosen's sake, if it be thy Will, send me Life and Health, that I may truly serve thee. O my Lord bless thy People, and save thine Inheritance. O Lord God save thy chosen People of England . O my Lord God, defend this Realm from Papistry, and maintain thy true Religion, that I and thy People may praise thy holy Name.

And therewithal he said, I am faint, Lord have mercy upon me, and take my Spirit. And so he yielded up to God his Ghost. July 6, 1553.

The *SHORTER*
CATECHISM
Compos'd by the
REVEREND ASSEMBLY of
DIVINES
At *WESTMINSTER.*

With Proofs thereof out of the Scriptures
Which are either some of the former-
ly quoted places, or others gathered
from their other *Writings*; all fitted
both for Brevity & Clearnefs, to this
their *Form of Sound Words.*
For the Benefit of Chriſtians in general, and of *Youth & Children* in un-
derſtanding in particular; that they
may with more eaſe acquaint themſelves with the *Truth* according to the
Scriptures, and with the *Scriptures*
themſelves.

Printed by *B. Harris,* and *J. Allen,*
and are to be Sold at the *London-
Coffee Houſe.* 1691

The SHORTER
CATECHISM

Agreed upon by the Reverend
Assembly of Divines *at Westminster.*

Question. **W**Hat is the chief End of Man?

Answer. Man's chief End is to Glorify God, and to Enjoy Him for ever.

Q2. *What Rule hath God given to direct us how we may glorify and enjoy Him?*

A. The Word of God, which is contained in the Scriptures of the Old and New Testaments, is the only Rule to direct us how we may glorify and enjoy him.

Q3. *What do the Scriptures principally teach?*

A. The Scriptures principally teach, what Man is to believe concerning God, and what duty God requireth of Man.

Q4. *What is God?*

A. God is a Spirit, Infinite, Eternal, and Unchangeable, in His Being, Wisdom, Power, Holiness, Justice, Goodness and Truth.

Q5. *Are there more Gods than One?*

A. There is but ONE only, the living and true God.

Q6. *How many Persons are there in the God-head?*

A. There are Three Persons in the Godhead; the Father, the Son, & the Holy Ghost; & these Three are One GOD the same in Substance, equal in Power & Glory.

Q7. *What are the Decrees of God?*
A. The Decrees of God are his eternal Purpose, according to the Counsel of his own Will, whereby, for his own Glory, he hath foreordained whatsoever comes to pass.

Q8. *How doth God execute his Decrees?*
A. God executeth his Decrees in the Works of Creation & Providence.

Q9. *What is the Work of Creation?*
A. The Work of Creation is God's Making all things of Nothing, by the Word of his Power, in the space of six days, et all very good.

Q10. *How did God create man?*
A. God created Man Male and Female, after his own Image, in Knowledge, Righteousness and Holiness, with Dominion over the Creatures.

Q11. *What are God's Works of Provi-dence?*

A. God's Works of Providence are his most holy, wise & powerful preserving & governing all his Creatures and all their Actions.

Q12. *What special Act of Providence did God exercise toward Man in the Estate wherein he was created?*

A. When God had created Man, He entered into a Covenant of Life with him, upon condition of perfect Obedience; forbidding him to Eat of the Tree of the knowledge of good and evil, upon pain of Death.

Q13. *Did our first Parents continue in the estate wherein they were created?*

A. Our first Parents being left to the freedom of their own Will, fell from the estate wherein they were created, by sinning against God.

Q14. *What is Sin?*

A. Sin is any want of Conformity unto, or Transgression of the Law of God.

Q15. *What was the Sin whereby our first Parents fell from the estate wherein they were created?*

A. The Sin whereby our first Parents fell from the estate wherein they were created, was their eating the forbidden fruit.

Q16. *Did all Mankind fall in Adam's first transgression?*

A. The Covenant being made with *Adam*, not only for himself but for his Posterity; all Mankind descending from him by ordinary Generation, sinned in him, & fell with him, in his first transgression.

Q17. *Into what estate did the Fall bring Mankind?*

A. The Fall brought Mankind into an estate of Sin and Misery.

Q18. *Wherein consists the sinfulness of that estate whereinto Man fell?*

A. The sinfulness of that estate whereinto Man fell, consists in the Guilt of *Adam*'s first Sin, the want of Original Righteousness, and the Corruption of his whole Nature, which is commonly called Original Sin, together with all actual Transgressions which proceed from it.

Q19. *What is the misery of that estate whereinto man fell?*

A. All Mankind by their fall, lost Communion with God, are under his Wrath & Curse, and so made liable to all the Miseries in this life, to Death it self, and to the pains of Hell for ever.

Q20. *Did God leave all Mankind to perish in the estate of Sin & Misery?*

A. God having, out of his meer good pleasure from all Eternity, Elected some to everlasting Life, did enter into a Covenant of Grace, to deliver them out of the State of Sin & Misery, and to bring them into a State of Salvation by a Redeemer.

Q21. *Who is the Redeemer of God's Elect?*

A. The only Redeemer of God's Elect, is the Lord Jesus Christ, who being the eternal Son of God, became Man, and so was, and continues to be God and Man in two distinct Natures, and one Person, for ever.

Q22. *How did Christ, being the Son of God become Man?*

A. Christ, the Son of God, became Man, by taking to himself a true Body and a reasonable Soul, being conceived by the power of the Holy Ghost, in the

Womb of the Virgin *Mary*, and born of her, and yet without Sin.

Q23. *What Offices doth Christ execute as our Redeemer?*

A. Christ as our Redeemer executes the Office of a prophet, of a Priest, and of a King, both in his estate of Humiliation & Exaltation.

Q24. *How doth Christ execute the Office of a Prophet?*

A. Christ executeth the Office of a Prophet, in revealing to us by his Word and Spirit, the Will of God for our Salvation.

Q25. *How doth Christ execute the Office of a Priest?*

A. Christ executeth the Office of a Priest, in his once offering up of himself a Sacrifice to satisfy Divine Justice,& reconcile us to God;& in making continual Intercession for us.

Q26. *How doth Christ execute the Office of a King?*

A. Christ executeth the Office of a King, in subduing us to himself in ruling and defending us, and in restraining and conquering all his and our Enemies.

Q27. *Wherein did Christ's Humiliation consist?*

A. Christ's Humiliation consisted in His being born, and that in a low condition, made under the law undergoing the miseries of *this life* the wrath of God, and the cursed Death of the Cross, in being buried and continuing under the power of Death for a time.

Q28. *Wherein consists Christ's Exaltation?*

A. Christ's Exaltation consisteth in his rising again from the Dead on the third day, in ascending up into Heaven, & sitting at the Right Hand of God the

Father, and in coming to judge the World at the last Day.

Q29. *How are we made Partakers of the Redemption purchased by Christ?*
A. We are made Partakers of the Redemption purchased by Christ, by the effectual Application of it to us by his Holy Spirit.

Q30. *How doth the Spirit apply to us the Redemption purchased by Christ?*
A. The Spirit applieth to us the Redemption purchased by Christ, by working Faith in us, & thereby uniting us to Christ in our effectual Calling.

Q31. *What is effectual Calling?*
A. Effectual Calling is the Work of God's Spirit, whereby, convincing us of our Sin & Misery, enlightning our Minds in the Knowledge of Christ, & renewing our Wills, he doth persuade & enable us to embrace Jesus Christ, freely

offered to us in the Gospel.

Q32. *What Benefits do they that are effectually called partake of in this Life?*

A. They that are Effectually called, do in this Life partake of Justification, Adoption, Sanctification, & the several Benefits which in this Life do either accompany or flow from them.

Q33. *What is Justification?*

A. Justification is an act of God's free Grace, wherein he pardoneth all our Sins, and accepteth us as righteous in his sight, only for the righteousness of Christ imputed to us, and received by Faith alone.

Q34. *What is Adoption?*

A. Adoption is an Act of God's Free Grace, whereby we are received into the Number, and have Right to all the Priviledges of the Sons of God.

Q35. *What is Sanctification?*

A . Sanctification is the Work of God's free Grace, whereby we are renewed in the whole Man, after the Image of God, & are enabled more & more to die unto Sin, & live unto Righteousness.

Q36. *What are the Benefits which in this life do accompany or flow from Justification, Adoption & Sanctification?*

A. The Benefits which in this Life do accompany or flow from Justification, Adoption and Sanctification, are assurance of God's love, peace of Conscience, joy in the Holy Ghost, increase of Grace, & perseverance therein to the end.

Q37. *What benefits do Believers receive from Christ at their Death?*

A. The Souls of Believers are at their Death made perfect in holiness, & do immediately pass into Glory; & their

Bodies being still united to Christ, do rest in their Graves till the Resurrection.

Q38. *What benefits do Believers receive from Christ at the Resurrection?*

A. At the Resurrection Believers being raised up to Glory, shall be openly acknowledged & acquitted in the Day of Judgment, & made perfectly blessed in the full enjoying of God, to all Eternity.

Q39. *What is the Duty which God requires of Man?*

A. The Duty which God requires of Man, is Obedience to his revealed will.

Q40. *What did God at first reveal to Man for the Rule of his Obedience?*

A. The Rule which God at first revealed to Man for his Obedience was the Moral Law.

Q41. *Where is the Moral Law summarily comprehended?*

A. The Moral Law is summarily comprehended in the Ten Commandments.

Q42. *What is the Sum of the Ten Commandments?*

A. The Sum of the Ten Commandments is, To love the Lord our God with all our Heart, with all our Souls, with all our Strength, and with all our Mind, and our Neighbour as ourselves.

Q43. *What is the Preface to the Ten Commandments?*

A. The Preface to the Ten Commandments is in these Words, *I am the Lord thy God, which have brought thee out of the Land of Egypt, out of the House of Bondage.*

Q44. *What doth the Preface to the Ten Commandments teach us?*

A. The Preface to the Ten Commandments teacheth us, that because

God is the Lord, & our God and Redeemer, therefore we are bound to keep all his Commandments.

Q45. *Which is the first Commandment?*

A. The first Commandment is, *Thou shalt have no other gods before Me.*

Q46. *What is required in the first Commandment?*

A. The first Commandment requireth us to know and acknowledge God to be the only true God and our God, and to worship and glorify him accordingly.

Q47. *What is forbidden in the first Commandment?*

A. The first Commandment forbiddeth the denying, or not worshiping and glorifying the true God, as God and our God, & the giving that Worship and

Glory to any other which is due to him alone.

Q48. What are we especially taught by these Words (Before me) *in the first Commandment?*

A. These Words (*Before me*) in the first Commandment, teach us That God who seeth all things, taketh notice of, and is much displeased with the Sin of having any other god.

Q49. Which is the Second Commandment?

A. The Second Commandment is, *Thou shalt not make unto thee any Graven Image, or any likeness of any thing that is in Heaven above, or that is in the Earth beneath, or that is in the Water under the Earth: thou shalt not bow down thy Self to them, nor serve them: for I the Lord thy God am a jealous God, visiting the Iniquities of the Fathers upon the Children, unto the third and fourth Generation of them that hate me, & showing mercy unto thousands of them that love me, and keep my Commandments.*

Q50. *What is required in the second Commandment?*

A. The second Commandment requireth the receiving, observing, & keeping pure & entire all such religious Worship & Ordinances, as God hath appointed in his Word.

Q51. *What is forbidden in the second Commandment?*

A. The second Commandment forbiddeth the worshiping of God by Images, or any other way, not appointed in his Word.

Q52. *What are the Reasons annexed to the second Commandment?*

A. The Reasons annexed to the second Commandment, are God's

Sovereignty over us, his Propriety in us, and the Zeal he hath to his own Worship.

Q53. *Which is the third Commandment?*

A. The third commandment is, *Thou shalt not take the name of the Lord thy God in vain: for the Lord will not hold him guiltless that taketh his Name in vain.*

Q54. *What is required in the third Commandment?*

A. The third Commandment requireth the holy & reverend use of God's Name, Titles, Attributes, Ordinances, Word and Works.

Q55. *What is forbidden in the third Commandment?*

A. The third Commandment forbiddeth all prophaning or abusing of any thing whereby God maketh himself known.

Q56. What is the Reason annexed to the third Commandment?

A. The Reason annexed to the Third commandment is, That however the Breakers of this Commandment may escape Punishment from Men, yet the Lord our God will not suffer them to escape his righteous Judgment.

Q57. Which is the fourth Commandment?

A. The fourth Commandment is, *Remember the Sabbath Day to keep it Holy. Six Days shalt thou labour & do all thy Work, but the Seventh Day is the Sabbath of the Lord thy God, in it thou shalt not do any work, thou nor thy Son, nor thy Daughter, thy Manservant, nor thy Maid Servant, nor thy Cattle, nor thy Stranger that is within thy Gates: for in Six Days the Lord made Heaven & Earth, the Sea, and all that in them is, & rested the Sev-*

enth Day: wherefore the Lord blessed the Sabbath Day, and hallowed it.

Q58. *What is required in the fourth Commandment?*

A. The fourth Commandment requireth the keeping holy to God such set times as he hath appointed in his Word; expressly one whole Day in seven, to be an holy Sabbath to Himself.

Q59. *Which day of the Seven hath God appointed to be the weekly Sabbath?*

A. From the beginning of the World to the Resurrection of *Christ*, God appointed the seventh Day of the Week to be the weekly Sabbath, and the first Day of the Week ever since, to continue to the end of the World, which is the Christian Sabbath.

Q60. *How is the Sabbath to be Sanctified?*

A. The Sabbath is to be sanctified by

an holy resting all that Day, even from such worldly Employments & Recreations, as are lawful on other Days; & spending the whole time in the public & private exercises of God's Worship, except so much as is to be taken up in the Works of Necessity & Mercy.

Q61. *What is forbidden in the fourth Commandment?*

A. The fourth Commandment forbiddeth the Omission or careless Performance of the Duties required, & the prophaning the Day by idleness, or doing that which is in itself sinful, or by unnecessary Thoughts, Words or Works, about our worldly Employments or Recreations.

Q62. *What are the Reasons annexed to the fourth Commandment?*

A. The Reasons annexed to the fourth Commandment, are God's allowing us six Days of the Week for our own Employments, His challenging a special Propriety in the seventh, his own Example, and his blessing the Sabbath Day.

Q63. *Which is the fifth Commandment?*

A. The fifth commandment is, *Honour thy Father & thy Mother; that thy Days may be long upon the land which the Lord thy God giveth that.*

Q64. *What is required in the fifth Commandment?*

A. The fifth Commandment requireth the preserving the Honour & performing the Duties, belonging to every one in their several Places and Relations, as Superiors, Inferiors, or Equals.

Q65. *What is forbidden in the fifth Commandment?*

A. The fifth Commandment forbiddeth the neglecting or doing any thing against, the Honour and Duty which belongeth to every one in their several Places & Relations.

Q66. *What is the Reason annexed to the fifth Commandment?*

A. The Reason annexed to the fifth Commandment, is a promise of long Life & Prosperity, (as far as it shall serve for God's glory and their own good) to all such as keep this commandment.

Q67. *Which is the sixth Commandment?*

A . The sixth Commandment is, Thou shalt not kill.

Q68. *What is required in the sixth Commandment?*

A. The sixth Commandment requireth all lawful Endeavors to preserve our own Life, and the Life of others.

Q69. *What is forbidden in the sixth Commandment?*

A. The sixth Commandment forbiddeth the taking away of our own Life, or the Life of our Neighbour unjustly, and whatsoever tendeth thereunto.

Q70. *Which is the seventh Commandment?*

A. The seventh Commandment is, *Thou shalt not commit Adultery.*

Q71. *What is required in the seventh Commandment?*

A. The seventh Commandment requireth the preservation of our own, and our Neighbour's Chastity, in Heart, Speech & Behavior.

Q72. *What is forbidden in the seventh Commandment?*

A. The seventh Commandment forbiddeth all unchaste Thoughts, Words and Actions.

Q73. *Which is the eighth Commandment?*

A. The eighth Commandment is, *Thou shalt not Steal.*

Q74. *What is required in the eighth Commandment?*

A. The eighth Commandment requireth the lawful procuring & furthering the Wealth & outward Estate of our selves and others.

Q75. *What is forbidden in the eighth Commandment?*

A. The eighth Commandment forbiddeth whatsoever doth, or may unjustly hinder our own or our Neighbour's Wealth or outward Estate.

Q76. *Which is the ninth Commandment?*

A. The ninth Commandment is, *Thou shalt not bear false Witness against thy Neighbour.*

Q77. *What is required in the ninth Commandment?*

A. The ninth Commandment requireth the maintaining and promoting of Truth between Man and Man, and of our own, & our Neighbor's good Name, especially in Witness bearing.

Q78. *What is forbidden in the ninth commandment?*

A. The ninth commandment forbiddeth whatsoever is prejudicial to Truth, or injurious to our own or our Neighbour's good Name.

Q79. *Which is the Tenth Commandment?*

A. The Tenth Commandment is, *Thou shalt not covet thy Neighbour's House, thou shalt not covet thy Neighbour's Wife, nor his Manservant, nor his Maid Servant, nor his Ox, nor his Ass, nor any thing that is thy Neighbour's.*

Q80. *What is required in the tenth Commandment?*

A. The tenth Commandment requireth full Contentment with our own Condition, with a right & charitable frame of Spirit towards our Neighbour, & all that is his.

Q81. *What is forbidden in the tenth Commandment?*

A. The Tenth Commandment forbiddeth all Discontentment with our own estate, envying or grieving at the good of our Neighbour, and all inordinate motions & affections to anything that is his.

Q82. *Is any man able perfectly to keep the commandments of God?*

A. No meer man since the Fall is able in this Life perfectly to keep the Commandments of God, but daily doth break them in Thought, Word and Deed.

Q83. *Are all Transgressions of the Law equally heinous?*

A. Some Sins in themselves, & by reason of several Aggravations, are more heinous in the sight of God than others.

Q84. *What doth every sin deserve?*

A. Every sin deserveth God's Wrath and Curse, both in this Life, and that which is to come.

Q85. *What doth God require of us that we may escape his Wrath and Curse, due to us for sin?*

A. To escape the Wrath & Curse of God due to us for Sin, God requireth of us Faith in Jesus Christ, Repentance unto Life, with the diligent use of all the outward Means whereby Christ communicateth to us the benefits of Redemption.

Q86. *What is Faith in Jesus Christ?*

A. Faith in Jesus Christ is a saving

Grace, whereby we receive and rest upon him alone for Salvation, as He is offered to us in the Gospel.

Q87. *What is Repentance unto Life?*

A. Repentance unto life is a saving Grace, whereby a Sinner out of a true sense of his Sin, and apprehension of the Mercy of God in Christ, doth with grief & hatred of his Sin, turn from it unto God, with full purpose of, & endeavour after new Obedience.

Q88. *What are the outward & ordinary means whereby Christ communicateth to us the benefits of Redemption?*

A. The outward and ordinary means whereby Christ communicateth to us the benefits of Redemption are his Ordinances, especially the Word, Sacraments, & Prayer; all which are made effectual to the Elect for Salvation.

Q89. *How is the word made effectual*

to Salvation?

A. The Spirit of God maketh the Reading, but especially the Preaching of the Word an effectual Means of Convincing & Converting Sinners, and of building them up in Holiness & Comfort, through Faith unto Salvation.

Q9o. *How is the Word to be Read and Heard that it may become effectual to Salvation?*

A. That the word may become effectual to Salvation, we must attend thereunto with diligence, Preparation & Prayer, receive it with Faith & Love, lay it up in our Hearts, & practice it in our Lives.

Q9I. *How doth the Sacraments become effectual means of Salvation?*

A. The Sacraments become effectual Means of Salvation, not from any virtue in them, or in him that doth administer them; but only by the blessing of Christ, and the working of the Spirit in them that by Faith receive them.

Q92. *What is a Sacrament?*

A. A Sacrament is an holy Ordinance instituted by Christ, wherein by sensible Signs, Christ and the benefits of the New Covenant, are represented, sealed, and applied to Believers.

Q93. *Which are the Sacraments of the New Testament?*

A. The Sacraments of the New Testament are Baptism, and the Lord's Supper.

Q94. *What is Baptism?*

A. Baptism is a Sacrament, wherein the washing with Water in the Name of the Father, & of the Son, and of the Holy Ghost, doth signify and seal our ingrafting into Christ, & partaking of the benefits of the Covenant of Grace, and our Engagement to be the Lord's.

Q95. *To whom is Baptism to be administered?*

A. Baptism is not to be administered to any that are out of the visible Church, till they profess their Faith in Christ, and Obedience to Him, but the Infants of such as are Members of the visible Church are to be Baptized.

Q96. *What is the Lord's Supper?*

A. The Lord's Supper is a Sacrament, wherein by giving and receiving Bread & Wine according to Christ Appointment, His Death is shewed forth; and the worthy Receivers are not after a corporal and carnal Manner, but by Faith, made Partakers of His Body & Blood, with all his benefits, to their Spiritual Nourishment and growth in Grace.

Q97. *What is required to the worthy*

receiving of the Lord's Supper?

A. It is required of them that would worthily partake of the Lord's Supper, that they examine themselves of their Knowledge to discern the Lord's Body, of their Faith to feed upon Him, of their Repentance, Love, & new Obedience; lest coming unworthily, they eat and drink judgment to themselves.

Q98. *What is Prayer?*

A. Prayer is an offering up of our Desires to God, for Things agreeable to His Will, in the Name of Christ, with Confession of our Sins, and thankful Acknowledgment of his Mercies.

Q99. *What Rule hath God given for our Direction in Prayer?*

A. The whole Word of God is of use to direct us in Prayer; but the special Rule of Direction is that form of Prayer which Christ taught His Disciples, commonly called, *The Lord's Prayer.*

Q100. *What doth the Preface of the Lord's Prayer teach us?*

A. The Preface of the Lord's Prayer, which is, *Our Father which art in Heaven,* teacheth us to draw near to God with all holy Reverence and Confidence, as Children to a Father, able & ready to help us, and that we should pray with and for others.

Q101. *What do we pray for in the first Petition?*

A. In the first Petition, which is, *Hallowed be thy Name*, we pray that God would enable us and others to glorify Him in all that whereby he maketh himself known, and that He would dispose all things to His own Glory.

Q102. *What do we pray for in the 2nd Petition?*

A. In the second Petition, which is,

Thy Kingdom come, we pray that Satan's Kingdom may be destroyed, the Kingdom of Grace may be advanced, ourselves & others *bro't* into it, & kept in it, & that the Kingdom of Glory may be hastened.

Q103. *What do we pray for in the 3rd Petition?*

A. In the third Petition, which is, *Thy will be done in Earth, as it is in Heaven*, we pray that God by his Grace, would make us able & willing, to know, obey & submit to his Will in all things, as the Angels do in Heaven.

Q104.*What do we pray for in the 4th Petition?*

A. In the fourth Petition, which is, *Give us this Day our daily Bread,* we pray, that of God's free Gift we may receive a competent Portion of the good things of this Life, and enjoy his blessing with them.

Q105. *What do we pray for in the 5th Petition?*

A. In the fifth Petition, which is, *And forgive us our Debts, as we forgive our Debtors,* we pray, that God, for Christ's sake, would freely pardon all our Sins, which we are rather encouraged to ask, because by his Grace we are enabled from the Heart to forgive others.

Q106. *What do we pray for in the 6th Petition?*

A. In the sixth Petition, which is, *And lead us not into Temptation, but deliver us from Evil,* we pray, that God would either keep us from being tempted to Sin, or support and deliver us when we are tempted.

Q107. *What doth the Conclusion of the Lord's Prayer teach us?*

A. The Conclusion of the Lord's

Prayer, which is, *For thine is the Kingdom, and the Power, and the Glory forever, Amen,* teacheth us to make our encouragement in Prayer from God only, and in our Prayers to praise him, ascribing Kingdom, Power and Glory to him. And in testimony of our Desires, and Assurance to be heard, we say, AMEN.

THE
New English
TUTOR,
Enlarged ;
For the more easy
attaining the True
Reading of
ENGLISH,
To which is added
Milk for Babes
I VI
II VII
III VIII
IV IX
V X

Proverbs 22. 6. *Train up a Child in the way he should go: and when he is old, he will not depart from it.*

Chap. 23. 17, 18. *Let not your Heart envy sinners, but be in the fear of the Lord all the day long.*

For surely there is an end, and your expectation shall not be cut off.

Eph. 1. 1. *Children obey your Parents in the Lord, for this is right.*

Of Serving GOD.

1. *God will have no time to save us, if we find no day to serve Him.*

2. *Shall we have six days in seven, and God not one?*

1 Chron. 28. 9. *My son, know the God of your Father, & serve Him with a perfect heart, & with a willing mind, for the Lord searches all hearts.*

Now the Child being entered in his Letters and Spelling, let him learn these and such like Sentences by Heart, whereby be will be both instructed in his Duty, and encouraged in his Learning.

The Dutiful Child's Promises,

I Will fear GOD, and honour the KING.

I will honour my Father & Mother.

I will Obey any Superiours.

I will Submit to my Elders.

I will Love my Friends.

I will hate no Man.

I will forgive my Enemies, and pray to God
   for them.

I will as much as in me lies keep all God's

Holy Commandments.
I will learn my Catechism.
I will keep the Lord's Day Holy.
I will Reverence God's Sanctuary,
 For our GOD is a consuming Fire.

An Alphabet Of Lessons For Youth.

A Wise Son makes a glad Father, but a foolish Son is the heaviness of his Mother.

BEtter is a little with the fear of the Lord, than great treasure and trouble therewith.

COme unto CHRIST all ye that labour and are heavy laden, and He will give you rest.

DO not the abominable thing which I hate, saith the Lord.

EXcept a Man be born again, he cannot see the Kingdom of God.

FOolishness is bound up in the heart of a Child, but the rod of Correction shall drive it far from him.

GRieve not the Holy Spirit.

HOliness becomes God's House forever.

IT is good for me to draw near unto God.

KEep thy Heart with all Diligence, for out of it are the issues of Life.

LIars shall have their part in the lake which burns with fire and brimstone.

MAny are the Afflictions of the Righteous, but the Lord delivers them out of them all.

NOw is the accepted time, now is the day of salvation.

OUt of the abundance of the heart the mouth speaketh.

PRay to thy Father which is in secret, and thy Father which sees in secret, shall reward thee openly.

QUit you like Men, be strong, stand last in the Faith.

REmember thy Creator in the days of thy Youth.

SAlvation belongeth to the Lord.

TRust in God at all times ye people; pour out your hearts before him.

UPon the wicked God shall rain an horrible Tempest.

WO to the wicked, it shall be ill with him, for the reward of his hands shall be given him.

EXHort one another daily while it is called t o d a y, l e f t a n y o f y o u b e hardened through the deceitfulness of Sin.

YOung Men ye have overcome the wicked one.

Zeal hath consumed me because thy enemies have forgotten the words of God.

Choice Sentences.

1. Praying will make thee leave sin-ning, or sinning will make thee leave praying.

2. Our Weakness and Liabilities break not the bond of our Duties.

3. What we are afraid to speak before Men, we should be afraid to think before God.

The LORD's Prayer.

OUr Fa-ther which art in Hea-ven, Hal-low-ed be thy Name. Thy king-dom come. Thy will be done on Earth as it is in Hea-ven. Give us this day our dai-ly Bread. And for-give us our Debts as we for-give our Deb-tors. And lead us not in-to Temp-ta-ti-on, but de-li-ver us from e-vil, for thine is the King-dom, the Pow-er and the Glo-ry, for e-ver, A-MEN.

The CREED.

I Be-lieve in GOD the Fa-ther Almigh-ty. Ma-ker of Hea-ven and Earth. And in Je-sus Christ his on-ly Son our Lord, which was con-ceiv-ed by the Ho-ly Ghost, Born of the Vir-gin Mary, Suf-fer-ed under *Pon-ti-us Pi-late,* was cru-ci-fi-ed, Dead and Bu-ri-ed, He de-scen-ded in-to-Hell. The third Day he a-rose a-gain from the Dead; and as-cen-ded in-to Hea-ven, and sit-teth on the Right Hand of God the Fa-ther Al-migh-ty From thence he shall come to judge the quick and the dead. I be-lieve in the Ho-ly Ghost, the Ho-ly Ca-tho-lick Church, the Com-mu-ni-on of Saints, the For-give-ness of Sins, the Re-sur-rec-ti-on of the Bo-dy, and the Life E-ver-last-ing A-MEN.

The Ten Commandments.
Exod. XX.

GOD spake all these Words saying, I am the Lord thy God, which have brought thee out of the Land of Aegypt, out of the House of Bondage.

I. Thou shalt have no other gods before me.

II. Thou shalt not make unto thee any graven Image, or any likeness of any thing that is in Heaven above, or that is in the Earth beneath, or that is in the Water under the Earth; thou shalt not bow down thy felt to them, not serve them, for I the Lord thy God am a jealous God, visiting the iniquity of the Fathers upon the Children, unto the third and fourth Generations of them that hate me and shewing Mercy unto thousands of them that love Me and keep my Commandments.

III. Thou shalt not take the Name of the Lord thy God in vain, for the Lord will not hold him guiltless that taketh his Name in vain.

IV. Remember the Sabbath Day and keep it holy, six Days shalt thou labor and do all thy Work, but the seventh day is the Sabbath of the Lord thy God, in it thou shalt not do any work, thou nor thy Son, nor thy Daughter, nor thy Man Servant, nor thy Maid Servant, nor thy Cattle, nor the Stranger that is within thy Gates, for six Days the Lord made Heaven and Earth, the

Sea, and all that in them is, and rested the seventh Day, wherefore the Lord blessed the Sabbath Day and hallowed it.

V. Honor thy Father and thy Mother, that thy Days may be long upon the Land which the Lord thy God giveth thee.

VI. Thou shalt not Kill.

VII. Thou shalt not commit Adultery.

VIII. Thou shalt not Steal.

IX. Thou shalt not bear false Witness against thy Neighbor.

X. Thou shalt not covet thy Neighbor's House, thou shalt not covet thy Neighbor's Wife, nor his Man Servant, nor his Maid Servant, nor his Ox, nor his Ass, nor anything that is thy Neighbor's.

These Words which I command thee this Day shall be in thy Heart.

MR. *John Rogers*, Minister of the Gospel in *London*, was the first Martyr in Q. *Mary's* Reign, and was burnt at *Smithfield, February* the fourteenth, 1554. His Wife, with nine small Children, and one at her Breast, following him to the Stake, with which sorrowful sight he was not in the least daunted, but with wonderful Patience died couragiously for the Gospel of Jesus Christ.

*Some few Days before his Death, he writ
the following Exhortation to his Children.*

Give ear my Children to my words
　　whom God has dearly bought.
Lay up his Laws within your heart,
　　and print them in your thoughts.
I leave you here a little Book
　　for you to look upon
That you may see your Father's face
　　when he is dead and gone,
Who for the hope of heavenly things,
　　while he did here remain,
Gave over all his golden years
　　to Prison and to Pain.
Where I among my Iron Bands,
　　enclosed in the dark,
Not many days before my Death,
　　I did compose this Work,
And for Example to your Youth,
　　to whom I wish all good.
I send you here God's perfect Truth,

and seal it with my Blood.
To you, my Heirs of earthly Things,
     which I do leave behind,
That you may read and understand,
     and keep it in your mind,
That as you have been Heirs of that
     that once shall wear away,
You also may possess that part
     which never shall decay.
Keep always GOD before your eyes,
     with all your whole intent.
Commit no Sin in any wise,
     keep his Commandment.
Abhor that errant Whore of Rome,
     and all her Blasphemies,
And drink not of her cursed Cup,
     obey not her decrees.
Give honor to your Mother dear,
     remember well her pain,
And recompense her in her Age,
     with the like love again.
Be always ready for her help,
     and let her not decay.

Remember well your Father all,
 who would have been your stay.
Give of your Portion to the Poor,
 as Riches do arise,
And from the needy, naked Soul
 turn not away your eyes,
For he that does not hear the cry
 of those that stand in need
Shall cry himself and not be heard,
 when he does hope to speed.
If GOD has given you increase
 and blessed well your store,
Remember you are put in trust,
 and should relieve the poor.
Beware of foul and filthy Lust,
 let such things have no place.
Keep clean your Vessels in the Lord,
 that He may you embrace.
You are the Temples of the Lord,
 for you are dearly bought,
And they that do defile the same
 shall surely come to naught.
Be never Proud by any means,

build not your house too high,
But always have before your eyes
    that you are born to die.
Defraud not him that hired is,
    your labor to sustain,
And pay him still without delay,
    his wages for his pain.
And as you would another man
    against you should proceed,
Do you the same to them again
    when they do stand in need.
Impart your Portion to the Poor,
    in Money and in Meat,
And send the feeble, fainting Soul
    of that which you do eat.
Ask Counsel always of the wise,
    give ear unto the end,
And ne'er refuse the sweet rebuke
    of him that is your Friend.
Be always thankful to the Lord,
    with Prayer and with Praise,
Begging of him to bless your work,
    and to direct your ways.

Seek first, I say, the living GOD,
 and always him adore,
And then be sure that he will bless
 your basket and your store.
And I beseech almighty God
 replenish you with Grace,
That I may meet you in the Heav'ns,
 and see you face to face.
And though the Fire my Body burns,
 contrary to my kind,
That I cannot enjoy your love,
 according to my mind,
Yet I do hope that when the Heav'ns
 shall vanish like a scroll,
I shall see you in perfect shape,
 in Body and in Soul.
And that I may enjoy your love,
 and you enjoy the Land,
I do beseech the living LORD
 to hold you in his hand.
Though here my Body be adjudged
 in flaming Fire to fry,
My Soul I trust will straight ascend,

to live with GOD on high.
What though this Carcass smart a while,
   what though this Life decay,
My Soul I trust will be with GOD,
   and live in him for aye.
I know I am a Sinner born,
   from the Original,
And that I do deserve to die
   by my Fore-Fathers fall.
But by our Savior's precious Blood,
   which on the Cross was spilt,
Who freely offer'd up his Life,
   to save our Souls from Guilt,
I hope Redemption I shall have,
   and all that in Him trust,
When I shall see him face to face,
   and live among the Just.
Why then should I fear Deaths grim look,
   since Christ for me did die?
For King and Caesar, Rich and Poor,
   the force of Death must trie.
When I am chained to the Stake,
   and faggots girt me round,

Then pray the Lord my Soul in Heav'n
   may be with Glory crown'd.
Come welcome Death, the end of fears,
   I am prepar'd to die;
Those earthly Flames will send my Soul
   up to the Lord on high.
Farewel my Children to the World,
   where you must yet remain.
The Lord of Host be your defense
   till we do meet again.
Farewel my true and loving Wife,
   my Children and my Friends.
I hope in heaven to see you all,
   when all things have their end.
If you go on to serve the Lord,
   as you have now begun,
You shall walk safely all your days,
   until your life be   done.
God grant you so   to end your days
   as he shall think it best,
That I may meet you in the heavens,
   where I do hope to rest.

Duty Of Children Towards Their Parents.

God hath commanded saying, Honour thy Father and Mother, and whoso curseth Father or Mother, let him die the Death. *Mat. 15, 4.*

Children obey your Parents in the Lord, for this right. *Ephes. 6, 1.*

2. Honour thy Father and Mother, (which is the first Commandment with Promise).

3. That it may be well with thee, and that thou mayst live long on the Earth.

Children, obey your Parents in all Things, for that is well pleasing unto the Lord. *Col. 3, 20.*

The Eye that mocketh his Father, and despiseth the Instruction of his Mother, let the Ravens of the Valley pluck it out, and the young Eagles eat it. *Prov. 30, 17.*

Father, I have sinned against Heaven, and before thee. *Luke 15, 10.*
19. I am no more worthy to be called thy Son.

No man ever hated his own flesh, but nourisheth and cherisheth it. *Ephes. 5, 19.*

I pray thee let my Father and Mother come and abide with you, till I know what God will do for me. *I Sam. 22, 3*

My Son, help thy Father in his Age, and grieve him not as long as he liveth. *Ec-clus. 3, 12.*
13. And if his Understanding fail, have patience with him, and despise him not when thou art in thy full Strength.

Whoso curseth his Father or his Mother, his Lamp shall be put out in obscure Darkness. *Prov. 20, 20.*

Spiritual Milk

For AMERICAN BABES,

Drawn out of the Breasts of both *Testaments*, for their Souls Nourishment.

By JOHN COTTON.

Question. **W**HAT *hath God done for you?*
Ans. God hath made me, he keepeth me, and he can save me.

Q1. *What is GOD?*

A. God is a Spirit of himself & for himself.

Q2. *How many Gods be there?*

A. There be but One GOD in three Persons, the Father, the Son, and the Holy Ghost.

Q3. *How did God make you?*

A. In my first Parents holy and righteous.

Q4. *Are you then born Holy and Righteous?*

A. No, my first Parents sinned, and I in them.

Q5. *Are you then born a Sinner?*

A. I was conceived in Sin, & born in Iniquity.

Q6. *What is your Birth Sin?*

A. Adam's Sin imputed to me, and a corrupt Nature dwelling in me.

Q7. *What is your corrupt Nature?*

A. My corrupt Nature is empty of grace, bent unto Sin, only unto Sin, and that continually.

Q8. *What is Sin?*

A. Sin is a Transgression of the Law.

Q9. *How many Commandments of the Law be there?*   *A.* Ten.

Q10. *What is the first Commandment?*

*A .*Thou shalt have no other Gods before me.

Q11. *What is the meaning of this Commandment?*

A. That we should worship the only true God, and no other besides him.

Q12. *What is the second Commandment?*

A. Thou shalt not make to thyself any graven Image, &c.

Q13. *What is the meaning of this Commandment?*

A. That we should worship the only true GOD with true Worship, such as he hath ordained, not such as man hath invented.

Q14. *What is the third Commandment?*

A. Thou shalt not take the Name of the Lord thy God in vain, &c.

Q15. *What is meant by the Name of GOD?*

A. God himself & the good Things of God whereby he is known as a Man by his Name, and his Attributes, Worship, Word and Works.

Q16. What is it not to take his Name in vain?

A. To make use of God and the good things of God, to his Glory, and our own good, not vainly, not irreverently, not unprofitably.

Q17. Which is the fourth Commandment?

A. Remember that thou keep holy the Sabbath day.

Q18. What is the meaning of this Commandment?

A. That we should rest from Labour, and much more from play on the Lord's Day, that we may draw nigh to God in holy Duties.

Q19. What is the fifth Commandment?

A. Honour thy Father and thy Mother, &c.

Q20. Who are here meant by Father and Mother?

A. All our Superiors, whether in Family, School, Church, or Common Wealth.

Q21. What is the Honor due to them?

A. Reverence, Obedience, and (when I am able) Recompence.

Q22. What is the sixth Commandment?

A. Thou shalt do no Murder.

Q23. What is the meaning of this Commandment?

A. That we should not shorten the Life or Health of ourselves or others, but preserve both.

Q24. What is the seventh Commandment?
A. Thou shalt not commit Adultery.

Q25. What is the Sin here forbidden?
A. To defile ourselves or others with unclean Lusts.

Q26. What is the Duty here Commanded?
A. Chastity to possess our Vessels in Holiness and Honor.

Q27. What is the eighth Commandment?
A. Thou shalt not Steal.

Q28. What is the stealth here forbidden?
A. To take away another man's goods without his Leave, or to spend our own without Benefit to ourselves or others.

Q29. What is the Duty here Commanded?
A. To get our Goods honestly, to keep them safely, and spend them thriftily.

Q30. What is the ninth Commandment?
A. Thou shalt not bear false Witness, &c.

Q31. What is the Sin here forbidden?
A. To lie falsely, to think or speak untruly of ourselves or others.

Q32. What is the Duty here required?
A. Truth and Faithfulness.

Q33. What is the Tenth Commandment?

A. Thou shalt not covet, &c.

Q34. *What is the coveting here forbidden?*

A. Lust after the Things of other Men, and Want of Contentment with our own.

Q35. *Whether have you kept all these Commandments?*

A. No, I and all Men are Sinners.

Q36. *What are the wages of Sin?*

A. Death and Damnation.

Q37. *How then look you to be saved?*

A. Only by Jesus Christ.

Q38. *Who is Jesus Christ?*

A. The eternal Son of God who for our sakes became Man, that he might redeem and save us.

Q39. *How doth Christ redeem and save us?*

A. By his righteous Life and bitter Death, and glorious Resurrection to Life again.

Q40. *How do we come to have a Part & Fellowship with Christ in his Death & Resurrection?*

A. By the Power of his Word and Spirit, which brings us to Him, and keeps us in him.

Q41. *What is the Word?*

A. The Holy Scriptures of the Prophets and Apostles, the old and new Testament, the Law and Gospel.

Q42. *How doth the Ministry of the Law*

bring you toward Christ?

A. By bringing me to know my Sin, and the Wrath of God against me for it.

Q43. *What are you hereby the nearer to Christ?*

A. So I come to feel my cursed Estate and Need of a Saviour.

Q44. *How doth the Ministry of the Gospel help you in this cursed Estate?*

A. By humbling me yet more, and then rais-ing me out of this Estate.

Q45. *How doth the Ministry of the Gospel humble you?*

A. By revealing the Grace of the Lord Jesus in dying to save Sinners, and yet convincing me of my Sin in not believing on him, and of my utter Insufficiency to come to him, and so I feel myself utterly lost.

Q46. *How doth the Ministry of the Gospel raise you up out of this lost Estate to come to Christ?*

A. By teaching me the Value & Virtue of the Death of Christ, and the Riches of his Grace to lost Sinners by revealing the Promise of Grace to such, and by ministering the Spirit of Grace to apply Christ, and his Promise of Grace unto myself, and to keep me in him.

Q47. *How doth the Spirit of Grace apply Christ,*

his Promise of Grace unto you &keep you in him?

A. By begetting in me Faith to receive him, Prayer to call upon him, Repentance to mourn after him, and new Obedience to serve him.

Q48. *What is Faith?*

A. Faith is the Grace of the Spirit, whereby I deny myself, and believe on Christ for Righteousness and Salvation.

Q49. *What is Prayer?*

A. It is a calling upon God in the Name of Christ by the Help of the Holy Ghost, according to the Will of God.

Q50. *What is Repentance?*

A. Repentance is a Grace of the Spirit, whereby I loath my Sins, and myself for them, and confess them before the Lord, and mourn af-ter Christ for the Pardon of them, and for Grace to serve him in Newness of Life.

Q51.*What is the Newness of Life,or new Obedience?*

A. Newness of Life is a Grace of the Spirit, whereby I forsake my former Lust & Vain com-pany, and walk before the Lord in the Light of his Word, and in the Communion of Saints.

Q52. *What is the Communion of Saints?*

A. It is the Fellowship of the Church in the

Blessings of the Covenant of Grace, and the Seals thereof.

Q53. *What is the Church?*

A. It is a Congregation of Saints joined together in the Bond of this Covenant, to worship the Lord, and to edify one another in all his holy Ordinances.

Q54. *What is the Bond of the Covenant by which the Church is joined together?*

A. It is the Profession of that Covenant which God has made with his faithful People, to be a God unto them, and to their Seed.

Q55. *What doth the Lord bind his People to in this covenant?*

A. To give up themselves and their Seed, first to the Lord, to be his People, and then to the Elders & Brethren of the Church, to set forward the Worship of God & their mutual Edification.

Q56. *How do they give up themselves and their Seed to the Lord?*

A. By receiving thro' faith the Lord & his Covenant to themselves, and to their Seed, and accordingly walking themselves & training up their Children in the Ways of the Covenant.

Q57. *How do they give up themselves and*

their Seed to the Elders and Brethren?

A. By Confessing of their Sins, and Profession of their Faith, and of their Subjection to the Gospel of Christ; and so they and their Seed are received into the Fellowship of the Church and the Seals thereof.

Q58. *What are the Seals of the Covenant now in the Days of the Gospel?*

A. Baptism and the Lord's Supper.

Q59. *What is done for you in Baptism?*

A. In Baptism, the washing with Water is a Sign and Seal of my washing in the Blood and Spirit of Christ, and thereby of my ingrafting into Christ, of the Pardon and cleansing of my Sins, of my raising up out of Afflictions & also of my Resurrection from the Dead at the last Day.

Q60. *What is done for you in the Lord's Supper?*

A. In the Lord's Supper, the receiving of the Bread broken and the Wine poured out is a Sign and Seal of my receiving the Communion of the Body of Christ broken for me, and of his Blood shed for me, and thereby of my Growth in Christ, and the Pardon and Healing of my Sins, of the Fellowship of the Spirit, of my strengthening and quickening in Grace, and of my sitting together with Christ on his Throne of Glory at the last Judgment.

Q61. *What was the Resurrection from the Dead, which was sealed up to you in Baptism?*

A. When Christ shall come in his last Judgment, all that are in their Graves shall rise again, both the Just and Unjust.

Q62. *What is the last Judgment which is sealed up to you in the Lord's Supper?*

A. At the last day we shall all appear before the Judgment Seat of Christ, to give an Account of our Works, and receive our Reward, according to them.

Q63. *What is the Reward that shall then be given?*

A. The Righteous shall go into Life eternal and the Wicked shall be cast into everlasting Fire with the Devil and his Angels.

Awake, Arise.

Awake, arise, behold thou hast
Thy Life a Leaf, thy Breath a Blast,
At Night lye down prepar'd to have
Thy sleep, thy death, thy bed, thy grave.

The Names and Order of the Books of the Old and New Testament.

*G*Enesis	*Ecclesiastes*
Exodus	Solomons Song
Leviticus	Isaiah
Numbers	Jeremiah
Deuteronomy	Lamentations
Joshua	Ezekiel
Judges	Daniel
Ruth	Hosea
I. Samuel	Joel
II. Samuel	Amos
I. Kings	Obadiah
II. Kings	Jonah
I. Chronicles	Micah
II. Chronicles	Nahum
Ezra	Habakkuk
Nehemiah	Zephaniah
Esther	Haggai
Job	Zechariah
Psalms	Malachi.
Proverbs	

Matthew
Mark
Luke
John
The Acts
Romans
I. Corinthians
II. Corinthians
Galatians
Ephesians
Philippians
Colossians
I. Thessalonians
II. Thessalonians
I. Timothy
II. Timothy
Titus
Philemon
Hebrews
James
I. Peter
II. Peter
I. John
II. John
III. John
Jude
Revelations.

The Numeral Letters And Figures, Which Serve For The Ready Finding Of Any Chapter, Psalm, And Verse In The Bible.

i	1	one
ii	2	two
iii	3	three

iv	4	four
v	5	five
vi	6	six
vii	7	seven
viii	8	eight
ix	9	nine
x	10	ten
xi	11	eleven
xii	12	twelve
xiii	13	thirteen
xiv	14	fourteen
xv	15	fifteen
xvi	16	sixteen
xvii	17	seventeen
xviii	18	eighteen
xix	19	nineteen
xx	20	twenty
xxi	21	twenty one
xxii	22	twenty two
xxiii	23	twenty three
xxiv	24	twenty four
xxv	25	twenty five
xxvi	26	twenty six
xxvii	27	twenty seven
xxviii	28	twenty eight

xxix	29	twenty nine
xxx	30	thirty
xxxi	31	thirty one
xxxii	32	thirty two
xxxiii	33	thirty three
xxxiv	34	thirty four
xxxv	35	thirty five
xxxvi	36	thirty six
xxxvii	37	thirty seven
xxxviii	38	thirty eight
xxxix	39	thirty nine
xl	40	forty
xli	41	forty one
xlii	42	forty two
xliii	43	forty three
xliv	44	forty four
xlv	45	forty five
xlvi	46	forty six
xlvii	47	forty seven
xlviii	48	forty eight
xlix	49	forty nine
l	50	fifty
li	51	fifty one
lii	52	fifty two
liii	53	fifty three

liv	54	fifty four
lv	55	fifty five
lvi	56	fifty six
lvii	57	fifty seven
lviii	58	fifty eight
lix	59	fifty nine
lx	60	sixty
lxi	61	sixty one
lxii	62	sixty two
lxiii	63	sixty three
lxiv	64	sixty four
lxv	65	sixty five
lxvi	66	sixty six
lxvii	67	sixty seven
lxviii	68	sixty eight
lxix	69	sixty nine
lxx	70	seventy
lxxi	71	seventy one
lxxii	72	seventy two
lxxiii	73	seventy three
lxxiv	74	seventy four
lxxv	75	seventy five
lxxvi	76	seventy six
lxxvii	77	seventy seven
lxxviii	78	seventy eight

lxxix	79	seventy nine
lxxx	80	eighty
lxxxi	81	eighty one
lxxxii	82	eighty two
lxxxiii	83	eighty three
lxxxiv	84	eighty four
lxxxv	85	eighty five
lxxxvi	86	eighty six
lxxxvii	87	eighty seven
lxxxviii	88	eighty eight
lxxxix	89	eighty nine
xc	90	ninety
xci	91	ninety one
xcii	92	ninety two
xciii	93	ninety three
xciv	94	ninety four
xcv	95	ninety five
xcvi	96	ninety six
xcvii	97	ninety seven
xcviii	98	ninety eight
xcix	99	ninety nine
c	100	an hundred

GOD'S Judgments On Disobedient Children.

2 Sam. 18. 9. ABsalom met the Servants of David, and Absalom Rode Upon a Mule, and the Mule went under the thick Boughs of a great Oak, and he was taken up between the Heaven and the Earth, and the Mule that was under him went away.

10. And a certain Man saw it, and told Joab, and said, behold I saw *Absalom* hanged in an Oak.

14. Then said Joab, I may not tarry thus with thee. And he took three Darts in his Hand, and thrust them through the Heart of Absalom, while he was yet alive in the midst of the Oak.

15. And ten Young men that bare *Joab's* Armour compassed about, and smote *Absa-*

lom, and slew him.

Upon Scoffing Children.

2 Kings **E**lisha went up from thence
2. 23. unto *Bethel* and as he was
going up by the Way, there came forth little
Children out of the City, and mocked him,
and said unto him, *Go up, thou Bald-head,
Go up, thou Bald-head.*

24. And he turned back and looked on
them, and cursed them in the name of the
Lord, and there came forth two She-Bears
out of the Wood, and tore forty and two
Children of them.

Upon Sabbath-breakers

Numbers **A**ND while the Children of
15. 32. *Israel* were in the Wilder-
ness, they found a Man that gathered Sticks

upon the Sabbath-day. 33. And they that found him gathering of Sticks, brought him unto *Moses* and *Aaron*, and unto all the Congregation.

34. And they put him in Ward because it was not declared, what should be done to him.

35. And the Lord said to *Moses*, the Man shall be surely put to Death, all the Congregation shall stone him with Stones without the Camp.

36. And all the Congregation brought him without the Camp, and stoned him with Stones, and he died as the Lord had commanded *Moses*.

Human Frailty.

OUR Days begin with trouble here,
    our Life is but a span,
And cruel Death is always near,

so frail a thing is Man.
Then sow the seeds of grace whilst young,
    that when thou com'st to die,
Thou may'st sing forth that triumph song,
    Death where's thy victory.

The Ten Commandments Put Into Short And Easy Rhymes For Children.

1. Thou shalt have no more gods but me.
2. Before no idol bend thy knee.
3. Take not the name of God in vain.
4. Dare not the Sabbath day profane.
5. Give both thy parents honor due.
6. Take heed that thou no murder do.
7. Abstain from words and deeds unclean.
8. Steal not, though thou be poor and mean.
9. Make not a wilful lie, nor love it.
10. What is thy neighbor's, dare not covet.

A Dialogue Between CHRIST, YOUTH., *And The Devil.*

YOUTH.

THose days which God to me doth send,
In pleasure I'm resolv'd to spend ;
Like as the birds in th' lovely spring,
Sit chirping on the bough, and sing ;
Who straining forth those warbling notes,
Do make sweet music in their throats,
So I resolve in this my prime,
In sports and plays to spend my time.
Sorrow and grief I'll put away,
Such things agree not with my day ;
From clouds my morning shall be free ;
And nought on earth shall trouble me.
I will embrace each sweet delight,
This earth affords me day and night:
Though parents grieve and me correct,
Yet I their counsel will reject.

Devil.

The resolution which you take,
Sweet youth it doth me merry make.
If thou my counsel wilt embrace,
And shun the ways of truth and grace,
And learn to lie, and curse and swear,
And be as proud as any are ;
And with thy brothers wilt fall out,
And sisters with vile language flout:
Yea, fight and scratch, and also bite,
Then in thee I will take delight.
If thou wilt but be rul'd by me,
An artist thou shalt quickly be,
In all my ways which lovely are,
Ther'e few with thee who shall compare.
Thy parents always disobey ;
Don't mind at all what they do say:
And also pout and sullen be,
And thou shalt be a child for me.
When others read, be thou at play,
Think not on God, don't sigh nor pray
Nor be thou such a silly fool,

To mind thy book or go to school ;
But play the truant ; fear not I
Will straitway help you to a lie,
Which will excuse thee from the same,
From being whipp'd and from all blame;
Come bow to me, uphold my crown,
And I'll thee raise to high renown.

YOUTH.

These motions I will cleave unto,
And let all other counsels go ;
My heart against my parents now,
Shall harden'd be, and will not bow:
I won't submit at all to them,
But all good counsels will condemn,
And what I list that do will I,
And stubborn be continually.

CHRIST.

Wilt thou, O youth make such a choice,
And thus obey the devil's voice !
Curst sinful ways wilt thou embrace,

And hate the ways of truth and grace ?
Wilt thou to me a rebel prove ?
And from thy parents quite remove
Thy heart also ? Then shalt thou see,
What will e'er long become of thee.
Come, think on God, who did thee make,
And at his presence dread and quake,
Remember him now in thy youth,
And let thy soul take hold of truth:
The Devil and his ways defy,
Believe him not, he doth but lie:
His ways seem sweet, but youth beware,
He for thy soul hath laid a snare.
His sweet will into bitter turn,
If in those ways thou still wilt run,
He will thee into pieces tear,
Like lions which most hungry are.
Grant me thy heart, thy folly leave,
And from this lion I'll thee save ;
And thou shalt have sweet joy from me,
Which shall last to eternity.

YOUTH.

My heart shall chear me in my youth,
I'll have my frolicks in good truth,
What e'er seems lovely in mine eye,
Myself I cannot it deny.
In my own ways I still will walk,
And take delight among young folk,
Who spend their days in joy and mirth,
Nothing like that I'm sure on earth:
Thy ways, O Christ ! are not for me,
They with my age do not agree.
If I unto thy laws should cleave,
No more good days then should I have.

CHRIST.

Woul'st thou live long and good days see
Refrain from all iniquity :
True good alone doth from me flow,
It can't be had in things below.
Are not my ways, O youth ! for thee,
Then thou shalt never happy be ;
Nor ever shall thy soul obtain,

True good, whilst thou doth here remain.

YOUTH.

To thee, O Christ, I'll not adhere,
What thou speak'st of does not appear
Lovely to me I cannot find,
'Tis good to set or place my mind
On ways whence many sorrows spring,
And to the flesh such crosses bring,
Don't trouble me, I must fulfil,
My fleshly mind, and have my will.

CHRIST.

Unto thyself then I'll thee leave,
That Satan may thee wholly have :
Thy heart in sin shall harden'd be,
And blinded in iniquity.
And then in wrath I'll cut thee down,
Like as the grass and flowers mown ;
And to thy woe thou shalt espy,
Childhood and youth are vanity ;
For all such things I'll make thee know

To judgment thou shall come also.
In hell at last thy soul shall burn,
When thou thy sinful race hast run.
Consider this, think on thy end
Lest God do thee in pieces rend.

YOUTH.

Amazed, Lord! I now begin,
O help me and I'll leave my sin:
I tremble, and do greatly fear,
To think upon what I do hear.
Lord! I religious now will be,
And I'll from Satan turn to thee.

Devil.

Nay, foolish youth, don't change thy mind,
Unto such thoughts be not inclin'd.
Come, cheer up thy heart, rouse up, be glad:
There is no hell ; why art thou sad ?
Eat, drink, be merry with thy friend,
For when thou diest, that's thy last end.

YOUTH.

Such thoughts as these I can't receive,
Because God's word I do believe ;
None shall in this destroy my faith,
Nor do I mind what Satan saith.

Devil.

Although to thee herein I yield
Yet e'er long I shall win the field
That there's a heaven I can't deny,
Yea, and a hell of misery :
That heaven is a lovely place
I can't deny ; tis a clear case ;
And easy 'tis for to come there,
Therefore take thou no further care,
All human laws do thou observe,
And from old customs never swerve ;
Do not oppose what great men say,
And thou shalt never go astray.
Thou may'st be drunk, and swear and curse,
And sinners like thee ne'er the worse ;
At any time thou may'n repent ;

'Twill serve when all thy days are spent.

CHRIST.

Take heed or else thou art undone ;
These thoughts are from the wicked One,
Narrow's the way that leads to life,
Who walk therein do meet with strife.
Few shall be saved, young man know,
Most do unto destruction go.
If righteous ones scarce saved be,
What will at last become of thee !
Oh ! don't reject my precious call,
Lest suddenly in hell thou fall ;
Unless you soon converted be,
God's kingdom thou shalt never see.

YOUTH.

Lord, I am now at a great stand:
If I should yield to thy command,
My comrades will me much deride,
And never more will me abide.
Moreover, this I also know,

Thou can'st at last great mercy show.
When I am old, and pleasure gone,
Then what thou say'st I'll think upon.

CHRIST.

Nay, hold vain youth, thy time is short,
I have thy breath, I'll end thy sport ;
Thou shalt not live till thou art old,
Since thou in sin art grown so bold.
I in thy youth grim death will send,
And all thy sports shall have an end.

YOUTH.

I am too young, alas to die,
Let death some old grey head espy.
O spare me, and I will amend,
And with thy grace my soul befriend,
Or else I am undone alas,
For I am in a woful case.

CHRIST.

When I did call, you would not hear,

But didst to me turn a deaf ear ;
And now in thy calamity,
I will not mind nor hear thy cry ;
Thy day is past, begone from me,
Thou who didst love iniquity,
Above thy soul and Saviour dear ;
Who on the cross great pains did bear,
My mercy thou didst much abuse,
And all good counsel didst refuse,
Justice will therefore vengeance take,
And thee a sad example make.

YOUTH.

O Spare me, Lord, forbear thy hand,
Don't cut me off who trembling stand,
Begging for mercy at thy door,
O let me have but one year more.

CHRIST.

If thou some longer time should have,
Thou wouldst again to folly cleave :
Therefore to thee I will not give,

One day on earth longer to live.

Death.

Youth, I am come to fetch thy breath,
And carry thee to th' shades of death,
No pity on thee can I show,
Thou hast thy God offended so.
Thy soul and body I'll divide,
Thy body in the grave I'll hide,
And thy dear soul in hell must lie,
With Devils to eternity.

The Conclusion.

Thus end the days of woful youth,
Who won't obey nor mind the truth ;
Nor hearken to what preachers say,
But do their parents disobey.
They in their youth go down to hell,
Under eternal wrath to dwell.
Many don't live out half their days,
For cleaving unto sinful ways.

Agur's Prayer.

REmove far from me Vanity and Lyes ; give me neither Poverty nor Riches, feed me with Food convenient for me.

Lest I be full, and deny thee, and say, Who is the Lord ? Or, at least I be poor and steal, and take the Name of my God in vain.

A GUIDE.

FOR THE

Child and *Youth*.

In Two Parts.

The First, for CHILDREN:
Containing plain and pleasant Directions
to read ENGLISH.
With Prayers, Graces, and Instructions
fitted to the Capacity of Children.

The Second, for YOUTH:

Teaching to Write, Cast Account, and
Read more perfectly.
With several other Varieties, both
pleasant and profitable.

by T. H. *M. A. Teacher of a private School*

London : Printed by *J. Roberts,* for the
Company of Stationers, 1725.

First In The Morning.

First in the Morning when though dost awake,
To God for his Grace thy Petition make, Some
Heavenly Petition use daily to say,
That the God of Heaven may bless thee alway.

New-England

PRIMER

Enlarged.

For the more eafy attaining
the true Reading of ENGLISH

To which is added,

The Affembly of Divines

CATECHISM.

BOSTON: Printed by S. Kneeland, &
T. Green, Sold by the Bookfellers. 1727.

Uncertainty Of Life

I in the Burying Place may see
    Graves shorter there than I;
From Death's Arrest no Age is free,
    Young Children too may die;
My God, may such an awful Sight,
    Awakening be to me !
Oh ! That by early Grace I might
    For Death prepared be.

What Good Children Must

    Good Children must,
Fear God all Day, Love Christ always,
Parents obey, In Secret Pray,
No false thing say, Mind little Play,
By no Sin stray, Make no delay,
    In doing Good.

Learn These Four Lines By Heart.

Have Communion with few.
Be intimate with ONE.
Deal justly with all.
Speak Evil of none.

THE

New-England

PRIMER

Enlarged.

For the more easy attaining the true
Reading of *ENGLISH*

To which is added,

The Assembly of Divines

Catechism.

BOSTON: Printed by T. Fleet,
and Sold by the bookfellers, 1737.

Portrait of King George II.

Now I Lay Me Down To Sleep.

Now I lay me down to sleep,
  I pray the Lord my soul to keep,
If I should die before I wake
I pray the Lord my soul to take.

Lord, If Thou Lengthen.

LORD, if thou lengthen out my days,
  Then let my heart so fixed be,
That I may lengthen out thy praise,
And never turn aside from thee.
  So in my end I shall rejoice,
In thy Salvation joyful be ;
My Soul shall say with loud glad voice,
Jehovah, who is like to thee ?
  Who takest the lambs into thy arms,
And gently leadest those with young,
Who savest children from all harms,

Lord, I will praise thee with my Song.
  And when my days on earth shall end,
And I go hence and be here no more,
Give me eternity to spend,
My God to praise for evermore.

VERSES For Little Children.

THOUGH I am young, a little one,
  If I can speak and go alone,
Then I must learn to know the Lord,
And learn to read his holy word.
'Tis time to seek to God and pray
For what I want for ev'ry day :
I have a precious soul to save,
And I a mortal body have.
Tho' I am young, yet I may die,
And hasten to eternity :
There is a dreadful fiery Hell,
Where wicked ones must always dwell ;
There is a heaven, full of joy,

Where godly ones will always stay.
To one of these in my soul must fly,
As in a moment when I die :
When God that made me calls me home,
I must not stay, I must be gone.
He gives me life, he gives me breath.
And he can save my soul from death,
By Jesus Christ, my only Lord,
According to his holy word.
He clothes my back and makes me warm ;
He saves my flesh and bones from harm ;
He gives me bread and milk and meat,
And all I have that's good to eat.
When I am sick, he if he please,
Can make me well, and give me ease ;
He gives me sleep and quiet rest,
Whereby my body is refresh'd.
The Lord is good and kind to me,
And very thankful I must be :
I must not sin as others do,

Lest I lay down in sorrow too :
For God is angry ev'ry day,
With wicked ones that go astray,
All sinful words I must refrain :
I must not take God's name in vain,
I must not work, I must not play,
Upon God's holy Sabbath day.
And if my parents speak the word,
I must obey them in the Lord,
Nor steal, nor lie, nor spend my days,
In idle tales and foolish plays.
I must obey my Lord's commands,
Do something with my little hands :
Remember my Creator now,
In youth, when time will it allow.
Young Samuel that little child,
He serv'd the Lord, liv'd undefil'd ;
Him in his service God employ'd,
While Eli's wicked children dy'd.
When wicked children mocking said,

To an old man, "Go up bald Head" ;
God was displeas'd with them, and sent
Two bears which them in pieces rent.
I must not like these children vile,
Displease my God, myself defile,
Like young Abijah, I must see,
That good things may be found in me.
Young King Josiah, that blest youth,
He sought the Lord, and loved the truth ;
He like a king did act his part,
And follow'd God with all his heart.
The little children, they did sing
Hosannah's to their heavenly King.
That blessed child young Timothy,
Did learn God's word most heedfully.
It seemed to be his recreation,
Which made him wise unto salvation :
By faith in Christ which he had gain'd
With prayers & tears that faith unfeign'd.
These good examples were for me,

Like these good children I must be.
Give me true faith in Christ my Lord,
Obedience to his holy word,
No word is in this world like thine,
There's none so pure, sweet and divine,
From thence let me thy will behold,
And love thy word above fine gold.
Make my heart in thy statutes sound,
And make my faith and love abound.
Lord circumcise my heart to love thee,
And nothing in this world above thee.
Let me behold thy pleased face,
And make my soul to grow in grace,
And in the knowledge of my Lord
And Savior Christ, and of his word.

Portrait of the Queen.

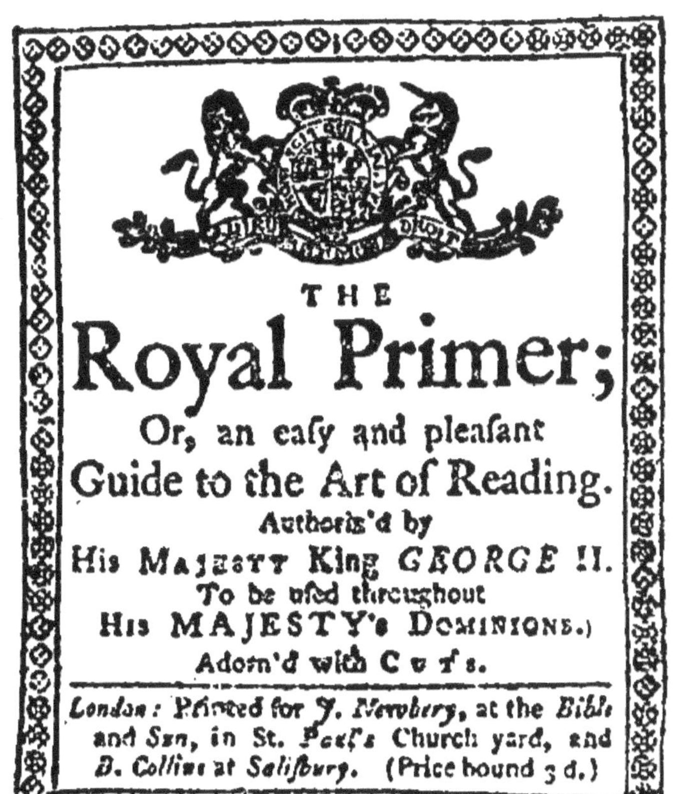

THE
Royal Primer;

Or, an eafy and pleafant
Guide to the Art of Reading.

Authoriz'd by

His MAJESTY King GEORGE II.

To be ufed throughout

His MAJESTY's DOMINIONS.)

Adorn'd with Cuts.

London: Printed for J. Newbery, at the Bible
and Sun, in St. Paul's Church yard, and
B. Collins at Salisbury. (Price bound 3 d.)

A Divine Song Of Praise To GOD, *For A Child, By The Rev. Dr.* WATTS.

HOW glorious is our heavenly King,
    Who reigns above the Sky !
How shall a Child presume to sing
    His dreadful Majesty !

How great his Power is none can tell,
    Nor think how large his Grace :
Nor men below, nor Saints that dwell,
    On high before his Face.

Nor Angels that stand round the Lord,
    Can search his secret will;
But they perform his heav'nly Word,
    And sing his Praises still.

Then let me join this holy Train;
    And my first Off'rings bring;
The eternal GOD will not disdain
    To hear an Infant sing.

My Heart resolves, my Tongue obeys,
    And Angels shall rejoice,
To hear their mighty Maker's Praise,
    Sound from a feeble Voice.

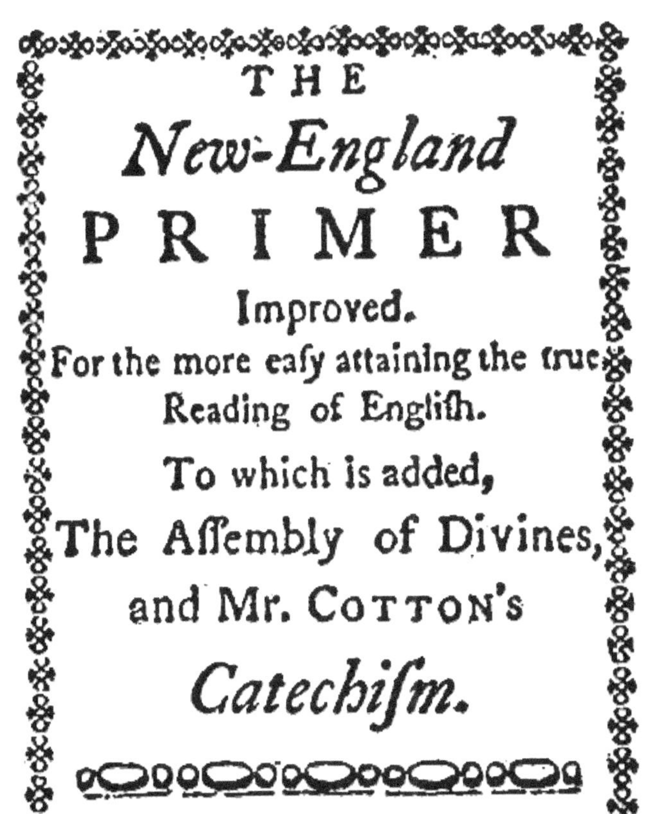

THE
New-England
PRIMER
Improved.
For the more eafy attaining the true
Reading of Englifh.
To which is added,
The Affembly of Divines,
and Mr. COTTON's
Catechifm.
BOSTON: Printed and Sold by
S. ADAMS, in *Queen-ftreet.* 1762.

Portrait of King George III.

Instructive Questions And Answers.

WHO was the first man ?	*Adam.*
Who was the first Woman ?	*Eve.*
Who was the first Murderer ?	*Cain.*
Who was the first Martyr ?	*Abel.*
Who was the first Translated ?	*Enoch.*
Who was the oldest Man ?	*Methuselah.*
Who built the Ark ?	*Noah.*
Who was the most faithful Man ?	*Abraham.*
Who was the meekest Man ?	*Moses.*
Who was the patientest Man ?	*Job.*
Who wrestled with the Angel of God ?	*Jacob.*
Who led *Israel* into *Canaan* ?	*Joshua.*
Who was the strongest Man ?	*Sampson.*
Who kill'd *Goliath* ?	*David.*
Who was the wisest Man ?	*Solomon.*
Who was in the Whale's Belly ?	*Jonah.*
Who saves lost Men ?	*Jesus Christ.*
Who is JESUS CHRIST ?	*The Son of GOD.*
Who was the Mother of Christ ?	*Mary.*
Who betrayed his Master ?	*Judas.*
Who denied his Master ?	*Peter.*

Who was the first Christian Martyr ? *Stephen.*
Who was chief Apostle of the Gentiles ?   *Paul.*

Some Proper Names Of MEN *And* WOMEN, *To Teach Children To Spell Their Own.*

Men's Names.

ADam, Abel,
Abraham, Amos,
Aaron, Abijah, Andrew,
Alexander, Anthony,
Bartholomew,
Benjamin, Barnabas,
Benoni, Barzillai,
Caleb, Caesar,
Charles, Christopher,
Clement, Cornelius,
David, Daniel,
Ephraim, Edward,
Edmund, Ebenezer,
Elijah, Eliphalet,
Elisha, Eleazer,
Elihu, Ezekiel, Elias,
Elizur, Frederick,
Francis, Gilbert,
Giles, George,
Gamalial, Gideon,
Gershom, Heman,
Henry, Hezekiah,
Hugh, John, Jonas,
Isaac, Jacob, Jared, Job,
James, Jonathan,
Israel, Joseph,
Jeremiah, Joshua,
Josiah, Jedediah, Jabez,
Joel, Judah, Lazarus,
Luke, Mathew,
Michael, Moses,
Malachi, Nathaniel,

Nathan, Nicholas,
Noadiah, Nehemiah,
Noah, Obadiah, Ozias,
Paul, Peter, Philip,
Phineas, Peletiah,
Ralph, Richard,
Samuel, Sampson,
Stephen, Solomon,
Seth, Simeon, Saul,

Shem, Shubal,
Timothy, Thomas,
Titus, Theophilus,
Uriah, Uzzah, Walter,
William, Xerxes,
Xenophon, Zachariah,
Zebdiel, Zedekiah,
Zadock, Zebulon,
Zebediah,

Women's Names.

ABigail, Anne,
Alice, Anna,
Bethiah, Bridget,
Cloe, Charity,
Deborah, Dorothy,
Dorcas, Dinah,
Damaris, Elizabeth,
Esther, Eunice,
Eleanor, Frances,
Flora, Grace,
Gillet, Hannah,
Huldah, Hepzibah,
Henrietta, Hagar.
Joanna, Jane, Jamima,

Isabel, Judith, Jennet,
Katharine, Katura,
Kezia, Lydia, Lucretia,
Lucy, Louis, Lettice,
Mary, Margaret,
Martha, Mehitable,
Marcy, Merial,
Patience, Phylis,
Phebe, Priscilla,
Rachel, Rebecca, Ruth,
Rhode, Rose, Sarah,
Susanna, Tabitha,
Tamefin, Ursula,
Zipporah, Zibiah

The Late Reverend And Venerable Mr. NATHANIEL CLAP, *Of* Newport *On* Rhode Island; *His Advice To Children.*

GOOD children should remember daily, God their Creator, Redeemer, and Sanctifier ; to believe in, love and serve him ; their parents to obey them in the LORD ; their bible and catechism ; their baptism ; the LORD's day ; the LORD's death and re- surrection ; their own death and resurrection ; and the day of judgment, when all that are not fit for heaven must be sent to hell. And they should pray to GOD in the name of CHRIST, for saving grace.

What's Right And Good.

WHAT's right and good now shew me Lord, and lead me by they grace and word. Thus shall I be a child of God, and love and fear they hand and rod.

The Infant's Grace Before And After Meat.

BLESS me, O Lord, and let my food strengthen me to serve thee, for Jesus Christ's sake.   AMEN.

I Desire to thank God who gives me food to eat every day of my life.   AMEN.

Advice To Youth. Eccle. Xii.

Now in the heat of youthful blood,
    Remember your Creator God ;
Behold the months come hast'ning on,
When you shall say, *My joys are gone.*

    Behold the aged sinner goes
Laden with guilt and heavy woes,
Down to the regions of the dead,
With endless curses on his head.

    The dust returns to dust again,
The soul in agonies of pain,
Ascends to God not there to dwell,

But hears her doom and sinks to hell.
  Eternal King I fear thy name,
Teach me to know how frail I am,
And when my soul must hence remove,
Give me a mansion in thy love.

The Sum Of The Ten Commandments.

WITH all thy soul love God above, and as thyself thy neighbour love.

Remember Thy Creator In The Days Of Thy Youth.

CHILDREN your great Creator fear,
  To him your homage pay,
While vain employments fire your blood,
  And lead your thoughts astray.
The due remembrance of his name
  Your first regard requires :
Till your breast glows with sacred love,
  Indulge no meaner fires.

Secure his favour, and be wise
   Before these cheerless days,
When age comes on, when mirth's no more,
   And health and strength decays.

Dr. WATTS'S *Cradle Hymn.*

HUSH, my dear; lie still and slumber,
   holy angels guard thy bed;
Heavenly blessings without number,
   gently falling on thy head.

Sleep my babe, thy food and raiment
   house and home thy friends provide,
All without thy care or payment,
   all thy wants are well supply'd.

How much better thou'rt attended
   than the Son of God could be,
When from heaven he descended,
   and became a child like thee.

Soft and easy is thy cradle,
   coarse and hard thy Savior lay,
When his birth-place was a stable,

and his softest bed was hay.

Blessed Babe ! what glorious features,
  spotless fair, divinely bright !
Must he dwell with brutal creatures,
  how could angels bear the sight !

Was there nothing but a manger,
  cursed sinners could afford
To receive the heavenly Stranger ;
  did they thus affront the Lord.

Soft my child I did not chide thee,
  tho' my song may sound too hard ;
'Tis thy mother sits beside thee,
  and her arms shall be thy guard.

Yet to read the shameful story,
  how the Jews abus'd their King,
How they serv'd the Lord of glory,
  makes me angry while I sing.

See the kinder shepherds round him,
  telling wonders from the sky ;
There they sought him, there they found him
  with his Virgin Mother by.

See the lovely Babe a dressing ;
   lovely Infant how he smil'd !
When he wept, his Mother's blessing
   sooth'd and hush'd the holy child.

Lo ! he slumbers in his manger,
   where the horned oxen fed ;
Peace my darling here's no danger,
   here's no ox a near thy bed.

'Twas to save thee, child from dying,
   save my dear from burning flame,
Bitter groans and endless crying,
   that thy blest Redeemer came.

May'st thou live to know and fear him,
   trust and love him all thy days !
Then go dwell forever near him,
   see his face and sing his praise.

I could give thee thousand kisses,
   hoping what I most desire :
Not a mother's fondest wishes
   can to greater joy aspire.

Our Saviour's Golden Rule.

BE you to others kind and true,
    As you'd have others be to you :
And neither do nor say to men,
    Whate'er you would not take again.

Duty To God And Our
Neighbour.

LOVE God with all your soul & strength,
    With all your heart and mind;
And love your neighbour as yourself,
    Be faithful, just and kind.
Deal with another as you'd have
    Another deal with you :
What you're unwilling to receive,
    Be sure you never do.

The Young INFANT'S *Or* CHILD'S *Morning Prayer. From Dr.* WATTS.

ALMIGHTY God the Maker of every Thing in Heaven and Earth ; the Darkness goes away, and the Day light comes at thy Command. Thou art good and doest good continually.

I thank thee that thou has taken such Care of me this Night, and that I am alive and well this Morning.

Save me, O God, from Evil, all this Day long, and let me love and serve thee forever, for the Sake of Jesus Christ thy Son.   AMEN.

The INFANT'S *Or Young* CHILD'S *Evening Prayer. From Dr.* WATTS.

O LORD God who knowest all Things, thou seest me by Night as well as by Day.

I pray thee for Christ's Sake, forgive me whatsoever I have done amiss this Day, and keep me all this Night, while I am asleep.

I desire to lie down under thy Care, and to abide forever under thy Blessing, for thou art a God of all Power and everlasting Mercy.   AMEN.

Some Short And Easy
Questions.

Q. WHO made you ?
A. God.

Q. Who redeemed you ?
A. Jesus Christ.

Q. Who sanctifies and preserves you ?
A. The Holy Ghost.

Q. *Of what are you made ?*
A. Dust.

Q. *What doth that teach you ?*
A. To be humble and mindful of Death.

Q. *For what End was you made ?*
A. To serve God.

Q. *How must you serve him?*
A. In Spirit and Truth.

The History Of Master Tommy Fido.

AS Goodness and Learning make the Child a Man, so Piety makes him an Angel. Master *Tommy Fido* not only loved his Book because it made him wiser, but because it made him better too. He loved every Body, and could not see a Stranger hurt, without feeling what he suffered, without pitying him, and wishing he could help him. He loved his Papa and Mamma, his Brothers and Sisters, with the dearest Affection ; he learnt his Duty to God, thanked him for his Goodness, and was glad that he had not made him a Horse or a Cow, but had given him Sense enough to know his Duty, and every Day when he said his Prayers, thanked God for making him a little Man. One Day he went to Church, he minded what the Parson said, and when he came home asked his Papa, if God loved him ; his Papa said Yes, my Dear. O! My dear Papa, said he, I am glad to hear it ; what a charming Thing it is to have God my Friend! Then nothing can hurt me ; I am sure I will love him as well as ever I can. Thus he every Day grew wiser and better. Every Body was pleased with him, he had many Friends, the Poor blessed him, and every one strove to make him happy.

THE
New-England
PRIMER
IMPROVED.

For the more eaſy attaining the
true Reading of Engliſh.

To which is added,

The Aſſembly of DIVINES

Catechiſm, &c.

B O S T O N:

Printed by W. M'Alpine, about Mid-
way between the Governor's and Dr.
Gardiner's, Marlborough-ſtreet. 1767

The History Of Creation.

In six Days God made the World, and all Things that are in it. He made the Sun to shine by Day, and the Moon to shine by Night. He made all the Beasts that walk on the Earth all the Birds that fly in the Air, and all the Fish that swim in the Sea. Each Herb, and Plant, and Tree, are the Works of his Hands. All Things both great and small, that live and move, and breathe in this wide World, to him do owe their Breath, to him their Life : And God saw all that he made, and all were good. But there was not a Man to till the Ground. So God made Man of the Dust of the Earth and breathed into him the Breath of Life ; and gave him rule o'er all that he had made : And the Man gave Names to all the Beasts of the Field, the Fowls of the Air, and the Fish of the Sea. But there was not found a Help meet for man ; so God brought on him a deep Sleep and then took from his Side a Rib, of which he made a Wife, and gave her to the Man and her Name was Eve : and from these two came all the Sons of Men.

A Collection Of The Best English Proverbs.

A friend in need is a friend indeed.
   Fair words butter no parsnips.
When the fox preaches let the geese beware.
   Fly the pleasure that will bite tomorrow.
If all fools wore white caps, we
   should look like a flock of geese.

A Short Prayer To Be Used Every Morning.

O LORD our heavenly Father, almighty and everlasting God, I most humbly thank thee for thy great mercy and goodness in preserving and keeping me from all perils and dangers of this night past, and bringing me safely to the beginning of this day ; defend me, O LORD, in the same, with thy mighty power ; and grant, that this day I may fall into no sin, neither run into any danger, but that all my doings may be ordered by thy governance, to do always that which is righteous in thy sight, through Jesus Christ our Lord.

AMEN.

A Short Prayer To Be Used Every Evening.

O LORD God, I beseech thee, of thy fatherly goodness and mercy to pardon all my offences, which in thought word or deed, I have this day committed against thee, and thy holy law. And now Lord, since the night is upon me and I am to take my rest, I pray thee lighten my eyes that I sleep not in death, let not my bed prove my grave, but so by the wings of thy mercy protect me, that I may rest from all terrors of darkness, that when I shall awake I may bless thy great and glorious name, and study to serve thee in the duties of the day following, that thou mayest be still my God, and I thy servant. Grant this for Jesus Christ's sake, to whom with thee and the Holy Ghost, be given, as most due, all honor and glory, now and forevermore.   AMEN.

Grace Before Meat.

O ETERNAL God, in whom we have our Being : We beseech thee bless with us these good Creatures provided for us, that in the strength thereof, we may set forth thy Praise and Glory, thro' Jesus Christ our Lord,
AMEN.

Grace After Meat.

THE God of Glory and Power, who hath created, redeemed, and at this time plentifully fed us ; Thy Holy Name be praised both now and evermore,   AMEN.

Advice To Children.

COME Babe most dear,
    To me draw near,
And harken to my Voice,
    My Counsel take,
    And thou shalt make
Thy Parents Hearts rejoice.
    Let true Love lead
    Thy Mind to read,
That thou may'st be a Preacher,
    To Slugs a Shame,
    To Blockheads blame,
But Gladness to thy Teacher.
    Be not as they
    Which follow Play,
With Dullards Head most muddy ;
    But let thy Mind,
    Be well inclin'd
Wisdom to seek with Study.
    For Fools do haste,
    Their Time to waste,
Spending in Sport the Day;

But while they jest,
Let thy Heart feast,
In seeking Wisdom's Way.
As God's dear Seed,
To learn give Heed.
That when thy Head is hoary;
Wisdom may be
A Crown to thee,
Transcending earthly Glory.
Do not dissemble,
But rather tremble,
With heart like broken Fallow;
Nor steal, nor swear,
But dread, and fear,
God's holy Name to hallow;
Nor lust, nor lye,
Lest thou should'st die
In such a woful State;
For God is just,
And all such must
Sink down into the Lake.
In God's own Way
Thou shalt obey,
Thy Father and thy Mother;

And as a Dove,
Shall live in Love.
With Sister and with Brother.
That in their Sight
Each Day and Night,
Thou may'st be Joy and Pleasure;
And in their Eye
Fixt constantly,
As their peculiar Treasure.
To each Delight,
In carnal Sight,
In God's pure Dread and Fear ;
My Soul doth yearn
That thou may'st learn
A slaying sword to wear.
To Christ's Cross bend,
And in the End,
Through Mercy, not as Merit,
In high Renown
And heavenly Crown,
And Kingdom shall inherit.
Thy Peace and Rest
From God's own Breast
Not Death or Hell shall fever :

But thou shalt see
Thy joy shall be,
Amen, in him for ever.

A Lesson For Children

Pray to God.
Love God.
Fear God.
Serve God.
Take not God's
Name in vain.
Do not Swear.
Do not Steal.
Cheat not in your play.
Play not with bad boys.

Call no ill names.
Use no ill words.
Tell no lies.
Hate Lies.
Speak the Truth.
Spend your Time well.
Love your School.
Mind your Book.
Strive to learn.
Be not a Dunce.

The *New-England* PRIMER

IMPROVED;

For the more eafy attaining the true Reading of ENGLISH.

TO WHICH IS ADDED,

The ASSEMBLY OF DIVINES, and Mr. COTTON'S CATECHISM.

PROVIDENCE:

Printed and Sold by JOHN WATERMAN, at the Paper-Mills, 1775.

Portrait of King George III.

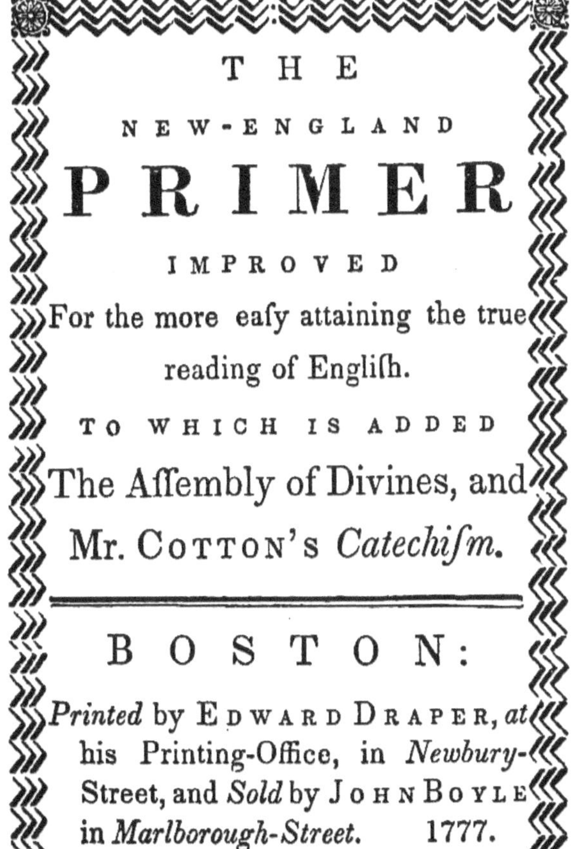

THE

NEW-ENGLAND

PRIMER

IMPROVED

For the more eafy attaining the true reading of Englifh.

TO WHICH IS ADDED

The Affembly of Divines, and Mr. COTTON's *Catechifm*.

BOSTON:

Printed by EDWARD DRAPER, *at* his Printing-Office, in *Newbury-Street*, and *Sold* by JOHN BOYLE in *Marlborough-Street.* 1777.

Portrait of John Hancock.

Portrait of Samuel Adams.

THE

NEW-ENGLAND

PRIMER,

ENLARGED AND IMPROVED;

OR, AN EASY AND PLEASANT

Guide to the Art of Reading.

ADORNED WITH CUTS.

ALSO THE

CATECHISM.

NEWBURYPORT:

PRINTED AND SOLD BY JOHN MYCALL.

Fear Thou The Lord

FEar thou the Lord and prize him more
   Than shining Gold and richest Oar :
For when thy Worldly Treasure's past,
The Fear of God will ever last.

A Little Boy And Girl At Prayers.

ALL good Boys and Girls say their Prayers every night and morning, and ask
their parent's blessing ; for which God Almighty loves and blesses them.

Good Boys At Their Books.

HE who ne'er learns his A, B, C,
Forever will a Blockhead be;
But he who his Book's inclin'd,
Will soon a golden Treasure find.

Children Like Tender Trees.

Children, like tender Trees do take the Bow,
And as they first are fashon'd always grow,
For what we learn in Youth, so that alone,
In Age we are by second Nature prone.

He that ne'er learns his ABC,
For ever will a Blockhead be ;

Alphabet Cuts (A-M)

But he that learns these Letters fair
Shall have a Coach to take the Air.

Alphabet Cuts (N-Z)

The   COCK.

The *Cock* doth crow to let you know
If you be wise, what Time to rise.

The   PARROT.

The *Parrot* prates he knows not what.
For all he says is got by Rote.

The NIGHTINGALE.

The *Nightingale* doth sweetly sing,
To welcome in the chearful Sprint.

The CUCKOW.

The Cuckow tells a merry Tale,
Upon the Hill, and in the Vale.

The   LAMB.

The little *Lamb* doth skip and play,
Always merry, always gay.

The   ASS.

The Ass, tho' mean, will by his Bray,
Oblige your Horse to run away.

The   LION.

The *Lion* ranges round the Wood,
And makes the lesser Beasts his Food.

The   WHALE.

The *Whale*'s the Monarch of the Main,
As is the Lion of the Plain.

The   BUTTERFLY.

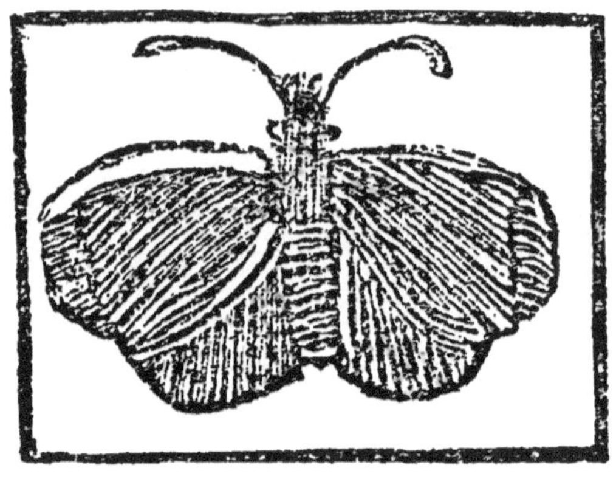

The *Butterfly* in gawdy Dress,
The worthless Coxcomb doth express.

The   CROCODILE.

The *Crocodile* with wat'ry Eyes,
O'er Man and every Creature cries.

Praise To GOD For Learning To Read.

THE Praises of my Tongue
    I offer to the LORD,
That I was taught and learnt so young
    To read his holy Word.
That I was brought to know
    The Danger I was in;
By Nature, and by Practice too,
    A wretched slave to sin.
That I am led to see
    I can do nothing well;

And whither shall a Sinner flee,
    To save himself from Hell.
Dear LORD, this Book of thine
    Informs me where to go,
For Grace to pardon all my Sin,
    And make me holy too.
Here I can read and learn
    How CHRIST, the Son of GOD,
Has undertook our great concern;
    Our Ransom cost his Blood.
And now he reigns above,
    He sends his Spirit down,
To shew the wonders of his Love,
    And make his Gospel known.
O may that Spirit teach,
    And make my heart receive
Those Truths which all thy Servants preach,
    And all thy Saints believe !
Then shall I praise the LORD
    In a more chearful Strain,
That I was taught to read his Word,
    And have not learnt in vain.

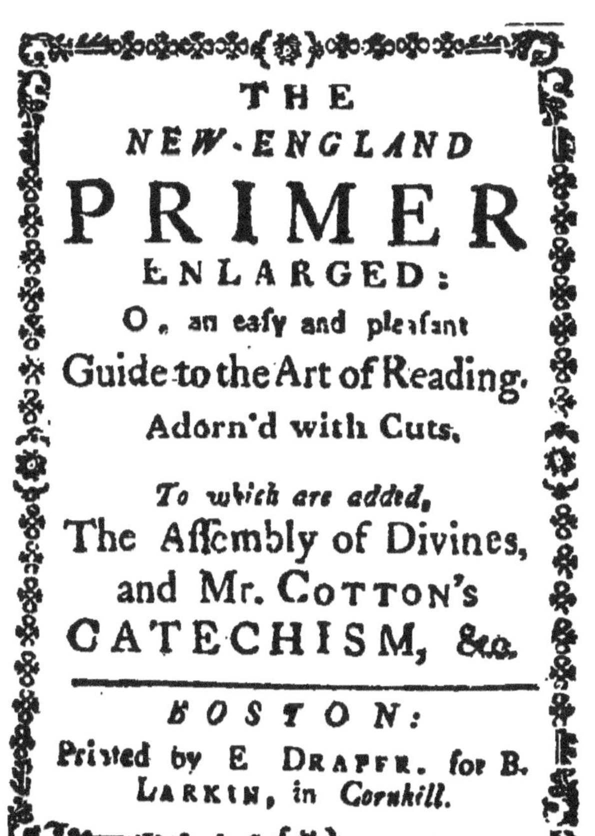
THE
NEW-ENGLAND
PRIMER
ENLARGED:
O, an easy and pleasant
Guide to the Art of Reading.
Adorn'd with Cuts.

To which are added,
The Assembly of Divines,
and Mr. COTTON's
CATECHISM, &c.

BOSTON:
Printed by E DRAPER. for B.
LARKIN, in Cornhill.

Portrait of George Washington.

THE

NEW-ENGLAND

PRIMER,

Or, an easy and pleasant

GUIDE to the ART of READING.

Adorn'd with CUTTS.

To which are added,

THE ASSEMBLY OF DIVINES'

CATECHISM.

BOSTON :—Printed and sold by
J. WHITE and C. CAMBRIDGE
near Charles River Bridge.

Portrait of George Washington.

Against Quarreling.

LET dogs delight to bark and bite,
　　For God hath made them so ;
Let Bears and Lions growl and fight,
　　For 'tis their nature to.
But children ! You should never let
　　Such angry passions rise ;
Your little hands were never made
　　To tear each other's eyes.

A Good BOY *And* GIRL *At Their Books.*

Children, like tender Osiers, take the bow,
And as they first are fashioned always grow :

For what we learn in youth, to that alone,
In age, we are by second nature prone.

A Little Boy And Girl Asking A Blessing Of Their Parents.

Adam And Eve.

Adam and Eve whilst innocent,
In Paradise were plac'd ;

But soon the Serpent by his wiles,
The happy pair disgrac'd.

ADAM had not been long in the garden of *Eden*, before God Almighty thought fit to increase his happiness, and considering he was alone, threw him into a deep sleep, and took out one of his ribs, from which he formed *Eve*, a more beautiful creature than himself, and allotted her to be a help-meet for him. *Adam*, at first sight of this new and lovely companion, cried out with extacy of joy, *Bone art thou of my bone, and flesh of my flesh*. In this happy state they lived but a short time ; for *Satan*, seeing their happiness, tempted the woman with the fruit of the tree of Knowledge, which God, to make trial of their obedience, had strictly charged them not to touch. The artful insinuations of the *Serpent*, together with the beauty of the fruit, prevailed on her to transgress the divine law. She tasted and was highly delighted so by her winning behaviour, tempted her husband to eat also. No sooner had they swallowed down the guilded bait, but their eyes were opened, they saw they were naked, and, conscious of their guilt endeavored to hide themselves in the garden from the wrath of their offended Creator ; but he soon drove them from their secret recess; turned them out of their secure bliss, and denounced thereupon not only a hard curse upon the *Serpent,* but on them likewise though with this ray of mercy in his anger said *the seed of the woman should bruise the serpent's head.*

A Morning Hymn.

MY God, who makes the sun to know
   His proper hour to rise,
And, to give light to all below,
   Doth send him round the skies :
When from the chambers of the east
   His morning race begins,
He never tires, nor stops to rest,
   But round the world he shines.
So like the sun would I fulfil

        The business of the day;
    Begin my work betimes, and still
        March on my heavenly way.
    Give me, O Lord, thy early grace,
        Nor let my soul complain
    That the young morning of my days
        Has all been spent in vain.

An Evening Hymn.

A ND now another day is gone,
        I'll sing my Maker's praise ;
    My comforts every hour make known
        His providence and grace.
    But how my childhood runs to waste !
        My sins, how great their sum !
    Lord, give me pardon for the past,
        And strength for days to come.
    I lay my body down to sleep,
        Let angels guard my head;
    And thro' the hours of darkness keep
        Their watch around my bed.
    With cheerful heart I close mine eyes,
        Since thou wilt not remove ;

And in the morning let me rise,
Rejoicing in thy love.

A Morning Prayer.

Now I wake and see the light :
'Tis God who kept me through the night ;
To him I lift my voice, and pray
That he would keep me through the day ;
If I should die before 'tis done,
O God accept me through thy Son.

On Life And Death.

Life and the *grave* two different lessons give;
Life shows us how to die, *death* how to live.

THE

NEW ENGLAND

PRIMER;

OR,

AN EASY AND PLEASANT GUIDE

TO

THE ART OF READING.

Adorned with Cuts.

TO WHICH IS ADDED

THE CATECHISM.

MASS. SABBATH SCHOOL SOCIETY,
Depository No. 13 Cornhill, Boston.
1843.

O Great Almighty God.

O GREAT Almighty God above,
Plant in my breast a fund of love,
That I thy mercies may adore,
And bless and praise thee evermore.

The Boy That's To His Book Inclined.

THE boy that's to his book inclined
Will soon a golden treasure find.

Offices Of Humanity.
Exodus XXII.

THOU shalt not see thy brother's ox or his sheep go astray, and hide thyself from them: thou shalt in any case bring them again unto thy brother.

And if thy brother be not nigh unto thee, or thou know him not, then thou shalt bring it unto thine own house, and it shall be with thee until thy brother seek after it, and thou shalt restore it to him again.

In like manner shalt thou do with his ass, and so shalt thou do with his raiment, and with all lost things of thy brother's, which he hath lost and and thou hast found, shalt thou do likewise thou mayest not hide thyself.

Thou shalt not see thy brother's ass or his ox fall down by the way, and hide thyself from them: thou shalt surely help him to lift them up again.

Lessons For Children.

Of The Fear Of God.

THEY that fear God least, have the greatest reason to fear him.

A fear of departing from God is a good means to keep us from departing from him.

The more we fear God, the less we shall fear men.

They that will not fear God in prosperity, will be afraid of him in adversity.

Means To Preserve Mercies.

1. BE thankful for them.
2. Receive them as mercies, not as dues.
3. Prepare to part with them.
4. Expect the continuance of mercies from God; he is the strength of our life, the staff of our bread, the breath of our nostrils, and the length of our days.

Of The Soul.

IT matters not what a man loses, if he saves his soul; but if he loses his soul, it matters not what he saves.

They that are least sensible of their souls wants are most miserable.

It is our greatest wisdom to be watchful over the frame of our spirit, to observe what helps it and what injures it.

If you lose your time, you lose your hopes; and if you lose your hopes, you lose your souls; and when your souls are lost, they shall never be ransomed: when your hopes are lost, they shall never be recovered; and when your time is lost, it shall never be redeemed.

Of Death.

THE longest life is a lingering death, First infancy dies, then childhood, then youth.

THE ABC BOTH IN LATIN AND IN ENGLISH

⟨ The . A B C both in Latin and in English.

✠ A b c d e f g h I j k l m n
o p q r s t u v w x y z   Amen.
a e i o u a e i o u
ab eb ib ob ub ba be bi bo bu
ae ee ie oe ue ca ce ci co cu
ad ed id od ud da de di do du
af ef ig of uf fa fe fi fo fu
ag eg if og ug ga ge gi go gu
In nomine patris et filii et spiritus
sancti.   Amen.   ¶ In the name of
the Father and of the Son and of
the holy ghost.   Amen.
Pater noster qui es in celis
sanctificetur nomen tuum
Adveniat regnum tuum
Fiat voluntas tua sicut
in celo et in terra.   Panem nostrum
quotidianum da nobis hodie.   Et
dimitte nobis debita nostra, sicut et

nos dimittim' debitoribus nostris.
Et ne nos inducas in temptatio-
nem. Sed libera nos a malo Amen.
OUr father which is in heaven
hallowed be your name. Let
your kingdom come to us. Your will
be fulfilled as well in earth as it is
in heaven. Give us this day our daily
food. And forgive us our offences, as
we forgive them that offend us. And
let us not be overcome by temptation
but deliver us from all evil.   Amen

AVe maria gratia plena dn's tecu
Benedicta tu in mulierib', et be-
nedictus fructus ventris tui Jesus.
HAil Mary, full of grace. Our
Lord is with thee. Blessed are
you among all women and blessed is
the fruit of your womb, Jesus. Amen.

CRedo in deu' patrem omnipo-
tentem creatorem celi et terre.

Et in Jesum christu' filiu eius vnicu dominu nostru. Qui coceptus est de spiritusancto natus ex maria virgine Passus sub poncio pilato: crucifixus mortuus et sepultus. Descedit ad in ferna, tertia die resurrexit a mortuis Ascedit ad celos sedet ad dexteram dei patris omnipotentis. Inde ven turus est iudicare viuos et mortuos Credo in spiritum sanctu, sanctam ecclesiam catholica',sanctor' co'muni onem, remissione' peccatoru', carnis resurrectione' et vitam eterna' Ame.

I Believe in God the Father almighty creator of heaven and earth. And in his only son Jesus Christ our Lord. Which was conceived by the Holy Ghost, and born of the virgin Mary. Which suffered under Pontius Pilate, and was crucified and died, and was buried.

And descended in to the hells, and rose again the third day from death to life.And ascended into the heav'ns and sits on the right hand of the father almighty. And shall come a gain and judge both quick and dead. I believe in the holy ghost, and the holy church catholic, the holy communion of saints, and the remission of sins, and the general resurrection of the body and soul, and everlasting life. Amen.   To help a priest to sing. **Confitemini dn'o quoniam bonus : quonia' in seculu' misericordia eius.**[1]

COnfiteor Deo, beatae Marie, omnibus sanctis et vobis, quia peccavi nimis cogitatione locutione et opere mea culpa. Precor sanctam Maria', oe's sanctos Dei et vos orare

---

1 *Confitemini...eius.* Praise the Lord, for He is good: for His mercy endures for ever.

pro me. Misereatur vestri omnipo
tens deus, et dimittat vobis omnia
peccata vestra: liberet vos ob omni
malo salvetet confirmet in bono et
perducat vos ad vita' eterna'.Amen[2].
Adiutorium nostrum in nomine domini. Qui fecit celum et terram. Sit
nomen dn'i benedictu'. Ex hoc nunc
et usque in seculu'[3]. Kyrye eleyson.
Xp'e eleyson. Kyrye eleyson[4].¶ Se

---

2 *Confiniteor...Amen*. Praise the Lord, for He is good:
for His mercy endures for ever. I confess to God,
blessed Mary, all the saints and you, that I have
sinned exceedingly by thought, word, and deed,
through my fault. I beseech Saint Mary, all the
saints, and you to pray for me. May almighty God
have mercy on you, and forgive you all your sins: deliver us from all evil, strengthen and confirm in good
and bring us to eternal life. Amen.

3 *Adiutorium...seculu*. Our help is in the name of the
Lord. Who made heaven and earth. Blessed be the
name of the Lord. Now and forever more.

4 *Kyrye eleyson...Kyrye eleyson*. Lord have mercy. Christ
have mercy. Lord have mercy.

quentia sancti evangelii secundum, Marcu', Matheu', Luca', Iohanne'. Gloria tibi dn'e. Per omnia secula seculoru'. Amen[5]. Dn's vobiscu'. Et cum sputuo. Sursum corda. Habe-mus ad dn'm. Gratias agam' dn'o deo nostro. Dignum et iustum est[6] Pax domini sit semper vobiscu'. Et cum spiritu tuo. Ita misse est. Deo gratias. Requiescat in pace. Amen[7].

¶Grace to be said before dinner.
BEnedicite. Dn's. The eyes of everything do look up, and

---

5 *Sequentia...Amen.* The holy gospels according to Mark, Matthew, Luke, and John. Glory be to God. For all generations. Amen.

6 *Dominus...semper vobiscu.* The Lord be with you. And with your spirit. Lift up your hearts. We lift them up to the Lord. Let us give thanks to the Lord our God. It is right and just.

7 *Pax...Amen.* The peace of the Lord be with you al-ways. And with you also. It is dismissed. Thanks be to God. Rest in peace. Amen.

they hope in the good Lord, and you give them their food in time convenient. You open your hand and do replenish every sensible creature with your benediction. Glory be to the father, to the son, & to the holy ghost. As it was in the beginning, and as it is now and ever shall be. Amen. Lord have mercy on us. Christ have mercy on us. Lorde have mercy on us. Our father, & etc. And let us not be overcome by temptation. But deliver us from all evil. Amen. Now let us all pray. Good Lord bless us and all your gifts which we shall receive of you by your bounteousness through Christ our lord Amen. O lord command you to bless. The king of eternal glory make us to be partners of the celestial meal. Amen. God is charity, and he that dwells in charity dwells in god, and god dwells in him. Let us pray that god may dwell in us, and that we may dwell in him. Amen.

⁋ Grace after dinner.

THe god of peace and love dwell always with us. O Lord have mercy on us. Thanks be to god. Good lord let all your works give knowledge to you, and let your holy saints give blessing to you.

Glory be to the father, etc.

We give thanks to the almighty god for all your universal gifts & benefits which lives & reigns as go through out all the world of worlds. Amen.

O all you nations laud you the lord. And all you people praise you him. Because his mercy is conferred on us and the truth of our Lord both remain eternally. Glory be to, etc.

Lord have mercy on us. Christ have mercy on us. Lord have mercy on us. Our father which art, etc. Christ did distribute goods, & gave it to the poor. His justice abides in the world of worlds. I shall bless our Lord in every time. His praise be evermore in my mouth. My soul shall be praised in our Lord. Let them that be gentle hear, & they shall thereof be glad. Magnify you the Lord with me, and let us exalt his name within him self. Blessed be the name of our lord from the beginning.   Now, and ever through out the world. Hail Mary. Now let us pray. Vouchsafe you lord god to give eternal life to all people doing good to us for your holy name Amen Let us bless our Lord. Thanks be to our Lord God. God grant that the souls of all faithful people departed out of this world, by his mercy may rest in eternal life. Amen. God preserve his church universal. And

this church of england special. And the supreme heed thereof our king. And grant us the bliss without ending. Amen.
¶ Grace for fish days.
Benedicite. Dominus.   God grant that they that are poor in spirit may feed and they shall be satisfied: they that seek him, their hearts and minds shall live in the world of worlds. Glory be to etc. Lord have mercy on us, etc. Our father which art.   Let us pray etc. Good lord bless us, etc. O lord command you to bless. The eternal king of glory refresh us with the meat of your spiritual food. The grace of our Lord Jesus Christ the charity of God, the communion of the holy ghost, be ever with us all. Amen. Break to the hungry your bread. And bring the needy men and wandering men into

your house. When you see one bare cover him, and display not your own brother's body. Thus the almighty Lord says.

¶ Grace for after dinner.

THe God of peace and of love dwell always with us. The merciful god giver of mercy has made a memory of his marvels. He has given meat to all them that dread him.   Glory be to the father. We give thanks to you, etc.

¶ A short grace to be said before dinner.

THe right hand of God bless our meat now brought hither and to be brought hither.   In the name of the father, and the son, etc.

¶ An other grace to be said before dinner or supper.

BEnedicite. Dn's.   Good Lord for your grace meekly we call.

Bless us our meats and drinks all.
In the name of the father, et cetera.
     ¶ A short grace after dinner.
For this feast now let us bless
our lord.   Thanks be to god.
Hail Mary, etc. Now let us all pray,
etc. Vouchsafe, etc. Let us all bless
our Lord. Thanks be to god. God
grant, etc. God preserve, etc.
     ¶ An other grace to be said
          after dinner or supper.
Blessed be our Lord which of
his grace. Has lent us our food,
good time, and space. Lord have
mercy on us. Christ have mercy, etc.
Thanks be to god. Laud and praise,
honor, and glory. Be to that lord
that reigns on high. Whose great
mercy is ever ready. To all them
that for it call. Therefore laud be to
him eternal. Now blessed be the
name of our lord. Now and ever

through out the world. Amen. God
preserve his church universal, etc.
¶ Grace before supper.

BEnedicite. Dominus. He that
gives all things, now sanctify
our supper. In the name of, etc.
¶ Grace after supper.

BEnedicite. Dominus. Blessed
is god in all his gifts, and holy
in all his works. Let him be our help
in the name of God which has made
heaven and earth.
Blessed be the name, etc. Vouch, etc.
¶ Grace at Easter before dinner.

BEnedicite. Dn's. This is the
day which our Lord made, let
us enjoy and be glad in the same. Glory be to the, etc. Lord have mercy on
us, etc. And let us not, etc. Now let
us, etc. Good Lord, etc. O Lord,
etc. The king of, etc. Cast you out
clean the old leaven that you may be

new dough as you are the sweet bread, for Christ our Easter Lamb is offered for us, therefore let us feed in our Lord. Amen.

⁋ Grace after dinner at Easter.

COnfess yourselves in the god of heaven which gives food to every sensible creature. O thou good lord, etc. Thanks be to god. O all ye nations laud ye the lord Because his mercy is confirmed on us, etc. Glory be to the father, etc. O Christ, in your resurrection the heavens and the earth be glad.

⁋ Let us pray.

GOod lord infuse the spirit of your charity in us, that by your pity you may make us agreeable to those things which you have made by your holy paschal Sacraments. By that same our Lord Jesus Christ your son which lives & reigns with you as god

in the unity of the same holy spirit
by all the world of worlds. Amen.
¶ The ten commandments.
Lord grant me grace to honor the
One god and never to swear in vain
The holy day to be kept by me.
My parents to obey and maintain
By thought nor deed no man to kill
To rob nor to steal no where
Nor to do lechery in act or will
Be no liar, nor false witness bear
Nor to defile my neighbor's wife
His lands, servants, or cattle
These ten precepts Lord all my life
Grant me grace I may keep well.
¶ The works of mercy bodily.
God give me grace the sick to visit
And give them meat that be hungry
To them that thirst drink to fetch
And prisoners to redeem and buy
To clothe the naked evermore ready
To poor wanderers to give lodging
And to bring the dead to burying

❡ The works of mercy ghostly.
God grant I may good counsel give
And teach them that ignorant be
To comfort them that be pensive
And to correct with charity
To suffer in all adversity
My neighbors trespass to forgive
And to pray for grace while I live
❡ The Capital sins.
Good lord grant me pride to forsake
And not to sin in covetous
Nor sloth, but in good works to make
Nor to be wrath nor furious
Nor disdainful nor envious
Nor for to sin in gluttony
Nor in no carnal Lechery.

Thus ends the A B C translated out
of Latin in to English with other
   devout Prayers.

❡ Imprinted at London in Paul's
Churchyard at the Sign of the
Maiden's Head by Thomas Petit.

www.ingramcontent.com/pod-product-compliance
Lightning Source LLC
Chambersburg PA
CBHW020914160726
47993CB00005B/1971